Children, Bereavement and Trauma

Children, Bereavement and Trauma

Nurturing Resilience

Paul Barnard, Ian Morland and Julie Nagy

Jessica Kingsley Publishers
London and Philadelphia

The right of Paul Barnard, Ian Morland, Julie Nagy and the contributors to be identified as authors of this work has been asserted by them in accordance with the Copyright, Designs and Patents Act 1988.

First published in the United Kingdom in 1999 by
Jessica Kingsley Publishers Ltd,
116 Pentonville Road, London
N1 9JB, England
and
325 Chestnut Street,
Philadelphia
PA 19106, USA.

www.jkp.com

© Copyright 1999 Paul Barnard, Ian Morland and Julie Nagy
Chapter 4 © Copyright 1999 Elizabeth Capewell
Chapter 8 © Copyright 1999 Liverpool Children's Project

Library of Congress Cataloging in Publication Data
A CIP catalog record for this book is available from the Library of Congress

British Library Cataloguing in Publication Data
Barnard, Paul
Children, bereavement and trauma : nurturing resilience
1. Bereavement in children
I. Title II. Morland, Ian III. Nagy, Julie
155.9'37'083

ISBN 1 85302 785 5

Printed and Bound in Great Britain by
Athenaeum Press, Gateshead, Tyne and Wear

Contents

Acknowledgements

We would like to acknowledge the thanks that we owe to all those people, too numerous to name individually, who became a part of the life of Liverpool Children's Project. This particularly includes all the children and young people who taught us over the years. Our thanks go to the students and volunteers who helped the Project survive on a shoestring, and to the Children's Society staff and managers who believed in this work. A special thanks to Roger Adams for making us think so hard!

A lot of work went into preparing this book in a short space of time. It goes without saying that if any errors or misrepresentations have crept into the text then these are entirely our fault and not those of the authors cited.

Ian Morland
December 1998

CHAPTER I

Setting the Scene
A Brief History of the Liverpool Children's Project

Paul Barnard and Ian Morland

> The claim of Liverpool Children's Project is to have developed a model of practice which does not pathologize children's reactions to trauma and bereavement, but recognizes the child's ordinary life as a place for recovery, growth and development.
>
> *Liverpool Children's Project, Action Plan 1995*

Our wish in this introduction is to set the scene for this book by describing its historical background, and so the origin of our work in Liverpool will be outlined. Our aim, throughout, is to share with the reader something of what we learned whilst working with bereaved children from 1989 to the closure of Liverpool Children's Project in June 1998. As well as working with children, we always aimed to disseminate information to other agencies and individuals: this book is an example of our efforts to do that. We hope readers will find something of value here for their own future work.

The opening quotation summarizes the claim which we made, to have found a novel way of working which helped children to cope whilst respecting their identity as *children* and not as clients or patients. Their identities – and their rights – as children are easily overlooked once the machinery of professionalism is wheeled out in response to an incident. One of Paul Barnard's early questions in undertaking bereavement work was, 'Where are the children in this?' – as adults coped in the aftermath of disaster, the children were easily overlooked. It is difficult for children to be heard and to have a say in their own lives even at the best of times. It is generally the adults who make decisions for them, with little dialogue or consultation. Imagine how much worse it can be when the child's carers are under pressure! It was in recognition of this reality that we sought a different method of working with bereaved children, to avoid making children feel even more powerless at a vulnerable time in their lives. To do this, we had to challenge the traditional roles of practitioner–client which are central to the encounter between professionals and those they help. We had to find ways of being alongside children and consider whether other people (the family, the school, etc.) in the child's life were better able to help. We were assisted in this by the recognition that children could use their innate ability to be resilient to trauma. We also recognized, out of listening to children themselves, that bereaved children did not inevitably need a bereavement service – some did and some did not.

We recognized from an early stage that our model of work could be widely applied: as a low-technology tool it is useful for working with young people with learning difficulties, and is certainly applicable to different kinds of trauma, including working with children who were affected by divorce, or with victims of bullying. The model was adopted for use in anti-bullying work by the Children's Society's Huyton Community Development Project in Merseyside. Our decision to concentrate exclusively on bereavement work was historical – the origins with a tragic disaster gave us a 'loyalty' to this work and to the demand for support which came from the communities around us.

Let us explain the historical context more fully. In April 1989, immediately after the Hillsborough disaster, which claimed 96 lives, the Children's Society seconded Paul Barnard to be involved in the network of support, based around the Hillsborough Centre in Liverpool. Paul's work was formally designated as 'The Hillsborough Project' in 1990. Paul worked with Amanda Martin as researcher/administrator until 1992. In that year, the service expanded and became 'Liverpool Children's Project' (LCP); Mandy left and Ian Morland and Gillian Moore joined the team. Gillian left in 1996; Julie Nagy joined the team in 1995. Throughout most of these years, there were continual contributions from Maureen Kane, as freelance educational consultant, to help with preparation and delivery of training workshops to educational and other professionals. Roger Adams, a research consultant employed by the Children's Society, was a mentor to the team's research and evaluation work. The Project also benefited from the contributions of a lively number of social work students and volunteers.

In addition to working with individuals, the Project always engaged in networking with other local agencies. In the 1989–91 period the closest contacts were with the Hillsborough Centre and with the Alder Centre at Alder Hey Hospital, regular meetings being held with the latter. Individual staff of Barnardo's worked with the Project, and particularly after 1996 a working relationship was established with Barnardo's Future Matters Project in Liverpool. All of these people and agencies made a contribution to our Project's process of learning.

Our work obviously originated in 'disaster work'. Over time, though, new demands emerged from the community – particularly from GPs and social workers who recognized a demand that they could not meet – and the focus of the work moved from supporting post-Hillsborough survivors to provision of support for children in the wake of other, individual and personal, tragedies. Since the launch of Liverpool Children's Project in April 1992, the Project addressed the experiences of children in acute trauma (following murder, suicide and road traffic accident) and bereavement caused by terminal illnesses in the family, in the context of their everyday lives. A consequence of recognizing that 'children's voices were not being heard' was that work began fairly soon to reach out to young children as well as to adolescents and young adults. Liverpool Children's Project eventually specialized in working with children aged under twelve because of the absence of support from elsewhere.

The term 'direct work' was used by LCP to describe the work which the Project undertook to support children, either individually or through small or large group activity work, following bereavement. The term originated from the dual strands of work which LCP undertook – working directly with bereaved children was one, and the other was to work 'indirectly' on behalf of children by providing information, workshops and structured training to adults who themselves worked with children, such as teachers and nursing staff.

Early learning points

In the early period of coping after Hillsborough, key points were learned from the experience of working with young people. They can be summarized briefly here as:

1. the value of listening and of listening uncritically;

2. the value of storytelling to somebody who has something they want or need to say;

3. the value of peer group support;

4. the need for all-inclusive support amongst friends and family and a recognition that professionals can only ever be present to help for a small portion of time;

5. the value of 'activity' or action for channelling feelings.

These five points provided an enduring legacy. They informed and came from a wider series of issues which were relevant in 1989 and to some extent are still true today.

Children and bereavement is still a taboo subject, surrounded by many myths and misunderstandings, but this social fact can be counterbalanced by 'the value of listening' by carers and professionals, and by 'the value of storytelling' by those in need of support.

In 1989 there was a lack of relevant literature and available research regarding the effects of disasters, trauma and bereavement on children, although more was being produced at that time as a result of the 1980s disasters – the *Herald of Free Enterprise* and others. One piece of literature which was influential, particularly in light of the community work perspective which was brought to this work, was *John Deere and the Bereavement Counselor* by Professor John L. McKnight. More will be said of this text later.

Because only some particular models of intervention have been promoted by bereavement specialists, the existing models are likely to pathologize the child and the whole experience of bereavement. They tend to pay more attention to adults' needs and perceptions than to children's needs. After the Hillsborough disaster, families expressed concern about the way they were being excluded from bereavement processes, as they had to make way for a process which was increasingly dominated by professionals and professional agencies. This is linked to 'the value of all-inclusive support' and a recognition that those who live with children in their everyday lives can be a valuable resource for support.

Children's voices were not being heard – perhaps because of lack of a safe space for them to tell their stories. Formal group work was regarded by some children as being unhelpful – they asked for 'something else' more 'normal'. This touched on the need for peer group support, and also for adults' acceptance of the need for young people to express themselves through action as well as through words.

Professional arenas and conferences were unlikely to pay attention to the needs of children and young people. This is a persisting truth: for example, at the National Institute of Social Work 'Disasters Conference' in June 1993, LCP was the sole contributor with regard to the needs and issues of children and young people following disaster, trauma or bereavement. Even in more recent years, as interest in children and trauma has increased, it has not necessarily been translated into child-friendly practice.

The above provides the professional context against which the work on resilience in children after bereavement and trauma was commenced. This began the process of 'action learning', carried out by workers on the ground and facilitated by Roger Adams. By use of action learning, the Project's practice evolved from reflecting on and evaluating the experience of working with children. This experience led to an understanding of their struggles with coping after events of bereavement or traumatic loss, and of how they seek to make sense of the experience.

CHAPTER 2

The Practice of Working with Bereaved Children

Julie Nagy

Group work has been the most visible and obvious example of how Liverpool Children's Project engaged with children, but in itself it tells only part of the story. The Project uses a range of approaches in working with children, including group activities and home visits and time spent with children individually. In this chapter I shall outline how a Project such as ours can engage with children from referral to leaving, and hopefully some ideas might be of use to those planning similar programmes.

Others who have organized successful group work will certainly have reached some similar conclusions to our own. It is important to think about how referrals will be made – and, how *can* they be made, how *should* they be made? There are questions of how workers manage to evaluate children's progress and how they enable children to evaluate this for themselves. And there are questions about the longer-term contact between a child and the Project, and the creation of opportunities for leaving and saying goodbye.

Our own intention from the beginning was to treat children as children and to respect their needs and their individuality. We did not wish to be prescriptive about what methods of working we would or would not use. Rather, the practice progressed because of the dialogue which we entered into with the children and our reflections on this. We learned to understand the struggle by children to cope after bereavement or traumatic loss, and how they seek to make sense of their experiences. Our work aimed to support children through their bereavement process, with activities such as using scrapbooks to help them store and keep memories of the dead person, role-play games to explore issues, more fun-centred day trips and holidays and video evenings, and creative and fun activities such as poetry workshops and the creating of the children's own magazine (ours was called *Shipshape*).

For some children, it can be a new and exciting adventure to go to a pantomime with their friends. These events can all provide a structured activity. The activities also provide opportunities which enable children to speak with an adult or other children about any issue to do with their experiences, to learn new things about themselves – what they can do, who they can be – and to re-establish their self-esteem and rebuild a sense of 'normality' and confidence in themselves. The range of aims can typically include:

1.   to support children, providing them with healthy coping strategies after the death of someone close to them;

2.   to listen to children and consider their needs;

3.   to talk to children;

4.   to make sure the children's voices are heard;

5.   to monitor and evaluate work and recognize when changes need to be made;

6.   to recognize the group work as part of a process which aims to facilitate for, and enable, the children.

This outline of how Liverpool Children's Project worked with children, from referral through to saying goodbye, is designed to be of use to those planning similar programmes.

Referrals typically came from a wide range of sources, including a quarter from families themselves who had learned of the Project through GPs or health visitors and others. Other referrals came directly through Social Services, schools, health visitors and GPs. So, perhaps not surprisingly, the main avenues were health, education and social services – the three statutory agencies which are most likely to be in contact with children. This has implications for the avenues chosen by other future workers to promote and advertise their bereavement services.

Initial discussion and the taking of details was usually by a telephone call from the family or another agency – e.g. their GP or a child's school or social worker. It was important to find out from the outset what the child's needs were likely to be and whether our service could meet these or not; for example, some contacts inevitably had to be referred elsewhere because of their nature or even because they were geographically too far away. There were also practical limitations: most bereavement services have to operate some kind of waiting list.

After this first contact, a standard procedure was followed when it seemed that LCP had something to offer. The process involved was to arrange a visit by a worker to meet with the child in the child's home, to send out an information pack about the Project and to send out a letter to explain what would happen during a visit. There should be time for the child and carer(s) to read through this material prior to the worker visiting. On a visit, workers would assess a child's needs – see Chapter 7, 'Planning Programmes of Work with Children', for examples of how these processes were designed.

It was important that, in line with the Project's philosophy, this visit focused on explaining the Project to the child, treating the child as a person able to make decisions rather than as if the worker's role was to offer an expert diagnosis and a prescription of what the child should be provided with. The children are thus encouraged to make decisions, not just to accept somebody else's decisions. In this way, from the outset we encouraged participation and sought to build self-esteem.

It sometimes became important to try to spend time with the child or children in a way which permitted them to speak with a worker whilst their carer was engaged in conversation with another worker; this permitted greater openness for the child and made discussion of their needs and interests easier. The worker would explain what the Project offered and why children came to groups (i.e. they had all had similar experiences), and explained that they had a choice about whether to come along or not. It was helpful to take along photographs of some of the group activities, to illustrate what the Project 'looks like' and to point out the workers, and it helped to show copies of children's work such as the *Shipshape* magazine.

The Project staff also found that adults in the family often required some support for themselves and were referred to appropriate agencies. The help given to children by LCP had a positive impact on families as a whole – but for those adults who needed their own support, we would make efforts to find local agencies which could provide this for them. LCP did organize occasional 'family' fun events for adults and children, but there was always a need to keep the focus of our work on the children. We prioritized our limited resources for their needs.

If a child is not interested in participating then this must be respected, although it must be (and was) made clear that they could phone the Project to talk with workers or to ask for advice, and that they could decide at a later date to begin to be involved in group activities. If a child was not interested in participating, the Project would nevertheless continue to be available to the child's carers, to offer them information or advice. This was obviously better than adding more pressure onto a child to attend group activities against his or her wishes. As with the adults, we would make efforts to find more appropriate services for a child if this is what they wanted; this could mean anything from referring to a counselling service, making contact with a local youth club, or identifying some other community facility.

If the child wished, they would be accepted onto our list of children with whom the Project worked – this meant that children would be regularly invited to activities. Communication was chiefly by post – each 3–4 months, a programme of activities was sent to children in a poster format, which they could hang on their bedroom wall (see Table 1.1 for an example). As a reminder, 'child-friendly' letters would be posted (addressed to the child, not the carer!) shortly before each event, often with a reply slip and a

SAE for return to the Project office. Phone calls from workers acted as a reminder of last resort (it is also important to remember that not all families were on the phone).

The nature, frequency and 'mix' of group activities changed over time as a result of action learning. Activities were, for example, targeted on different age ranges, such as 6–8 years and 9–12 years, to accommodate the needs of children using the Project at the time. Smaller groups, of no more than eight children, were used for more 'reflective' activities, such as creating scrapbooks to hold memories or the use of drama and role play, whilst larger numbers could be accommodated for more active events. Food was often provided as a part of the group activities, and where feasible the children could be involved in making snacks; children and families were informed in advance whether food was to be provided by LCP. Participating in preparing food, and certainly in the eating of it, is a very good way of engaging with most people.

Health and safety responsibilities and legal obligations needed to be observed, such as when participating in certain activities meant evening work or leaving Project premises and travelling by minibus. For days out and holidays, it is important to ensure that families know the phone numbers at which staff and their children can be contacted. A mobile phone is a good investment.

Where possible, carers and families were encouraged to bring the children to the venues. It was always necessary, though, for some children to be collected because of some families' transport difficulties. They were then collected by a worker who was known to them.

Table 2.1 An example of the kind of 'Activities Poster' which can be produced for use with children

Activity	Who for	Date	Place	Who will pick you up and drop you off	'I will be going'
INTRO FOR GROUP	Children	Nov 7	Merseyside House	Barney, Julie Gillian	
SHIPSHAPE	Children	Nov 14	Merseyside House	Barney, Karen	
ACTIVITY	Family	Nov 21		Your family	
WEEKEND AWAY	Children	Nov 23–24		Your family	
SCRAPBOOK	Children	Nov 28	Merseyside House	Barney, Susan	
CHRISTMAS CARDS	Children	Dec 5	Merseyside House	Derek, Gillian	
SCRAPBOOK	Children	Dec 12	Merseyside House	Derek, Karen	
CINEMA TRIP	Children	Dec 19		Barney, Karen, Susan	
PANTO	Family	Jan 11	Unity Theatre	Your family	
SHIPSHAPE	Children	Jan 16	Crown Street	Barney, Karen	
(HOME VISITS)		w/c Jan 23			
LEAVERS' PARTY	Children	Jan 30		Derek, Susan	
SCRAPBOOKS	Children	Feb 6	Crown Street	Derek, Gillian	
WEEKEND AWAY inc. Ship.	Children	Feb 15–16		Your family	
ACTIVITY	Children	Feb 20		Derek, Julie	
(INDIVIDUAL VISITS)		Feb 27			
SHIPSHAPE	Children	Mar 6	Crown Street	Barney, Susan	
ACTIVITY	Children	Mar 13		Derek, Karen	
WEEKEND AWAY	Children	Mar 20–23		Your family	
EASTER LEAVERS' PARTY	Children	Mar 27			

There are lots of blank spaces on your poster. This is because we would like you to think about the activities that you would like to do. We will ask you about this on November 7, so have a think about it and come with lots of ideas. Remember, one of us will ring you every Tuesday after school to find out if you are coming to the Project. You can tick your box on your poster (where the arrow is) to remind yourself if you are coming.

(*This final programme was organized in conjunction with Gillian Moore at Barnardo's*)

The Project operated a flexible policy regarding how long a period each child may continue to participate in group activities. We did not have a set period of time that children would come to the Project and then leave, so that the service could adapt to suit the very different circumstances of each child and family. This is not to say that children's progress was not evaluated, but it does mean that children with greater needs were either able to make use of the Project for longer periods, or else work was done to help them identify if they had needs which could be met in any other ways.

We did operate a simple system of recording which children came to which activities, and at times it was obvious that some children had not been attending on a regular basis. They were re-contacted, as their absence had been noticed, and we would check whether they had any worries or concerns and whether we could offer them anything. Perhaps they simply found the Project boring, but it was helpful to all involved if workers could find out!

The group activities were reviewed at the end of each 'season', with an eye on whether events were enjoyable and whether children would prefer to do other things. The children's progress was also reviewed in an informal but individual manner, involving workers talking with the child, and visiting them at home again and talking with the carer(s). We used standardized but simple questionnaires to gain children's views, as well as more conversational discussions when workers visited the children at home.

Leaving the Project was another transition for children, and had to be approached carefully. As and when children became ready to leave the Project's programme, this was negotiated with them during a series of home visits. The aim was to discuss their progress and feelings and to explain how LCP could help them to leave, e.g. by means of organizing a leavers' party for them, by giving them copies of the photographs of the activities which they had attended, and by ensuring that they could exchange phone numbers with other children to stay in touch with new friends. We would also help in finding other community-based activities and groups which could help them to develop their social interests further. When children did leave the programme, it was explained to them that they would not be invited to activities but could still contact us in the future. Where other pressures existed which hampered the family's and the child's resilience, the Project did sometimes become involved in liaising with other services to help to have these needs addressed.

CHAPTER 3

When Children are Involved in Disasters

Paul Barnard and Ian Morland

The work of Liverpool Children's Project began by working with children involved in disasters. Disasters have played a role in our own personal lives, to a greater or lesser extent – Paul and Julie's city experienced the Hillsborough disaster, whilst Ian's home town was twice bombed by the IRA. For us, disaster working has faded into the background and become memory. But disasters do still happen, whether as a result of organized terror, a lone madman, misadventure or human error. So it is important for a few basic suggestions to be outlined on the subject. This is, however, a large subject and can be touched on only briefly here.

One useful reference is to the work of Dr Ofra Ayalon, of the University of Haifa, Israel. Her book *Rescue! Community Oriented Preventative Education for Coping with Stress* (Ayalon 1988) is, we believe, currently out of print but may be available in university libraries. Although her work is set against the context of Israel and the Middle East conflict, many themes are just as relevant in Britain. Dr Ayalon touches on similar themes to our own, such as the importance of ensuring that children have a voice and are not disempowered after an incident. She places emphasis on healthy coping and the importance of resilience to enable children to cope with their experiences. She also suggests methods of preparation for events, so-called 'stress inoculation', which has probably been a relevant subject in Israel because of the conflicts of the past 30 years. In the UK, in 1993 a booklet was sent by the Gulbenkian

Foundation to every school: 'Coping with Crises in Schools – Wise Before the Event' by William Yule and Anne Gold.

Humour is perhaps an unusual consideration in approaching disaster work. Humour is a natural part of human behaviour that is often overlooked, and may seem particularly inappropriate in the context of tragedy or disaster. However, there are arguments in favour of acknowledging that humour can be used to help people cope with their experiences – for example the gallows humour of the person who feels that their situation is unbearable but has to be borne all the same. Humour has been examined by Carmen Moran and Margaret Massam (1997), and they comment that 'an important delineation needs to be made between a healthy use of humour and humour that is used to mask feelings in a way that will cause later distress'. Humour which directs anger and hurt towards another person can obviously be harmful, so as with any coping strategy it needs to be carefully used. If used without regard to the situation or if it impairs our social competence, it could actually cause more stress in those around us.

Amid the dozens of sociological and psychological comm- entaries on humour, it is probably safe to say that humour works because it is comforting; yet it can also be subversive, in that it helps us to cope with injustices and pain by challenging conventional views. Death and disaster are the taboos of our time, so we can speculate that humour comes to mind as a safe way to touch on taboo subjects. On the one hand humour may help to reframe a situation to make it more palatable; on the other it may simply assist in putting a little distance between the person and his/her situation.

Children may use humour after a disaster, but it may also be a release for those who work with them. Alexander and Wells in their study of police officers working on the Piper Alpha disaster reported that officers used humour to cope with their feelings but were aware that a joke or wisecrack quoted out of context would be deemed tasteless and offensive (Alexander and Wells 1991).

As suggested above, humour can be useful for services staff as well for disaster victims. Workers' health should not be overlooked.

As the American Red Cross has stated, disaster workers have the potential to become 'secondary victims', as they may find themselves working long, hard hours under poor conditions (see David Baldwin's Trauma Information Pages, http:// www. trauma-pages.com/). Personal support systems in the family may be left at home, some distance away. New working relationships and supports must be formed while involved in the support operation and while time is scarce. Administrative organization and managerial support is often created 'on the hoof', adding additional stress to workers who try to satisfy the needs of the service users and of the support service infrastructure.

One of the recurrent themes in literature on disasters is Critical Incident Stress Debriefing (CISD), particularly for emergency services personnel. Richard Grist and S. Joseph Woodall have made recent comments on these phenomena which share many common themes with John McKnight's critique of bereavement counselling (Grist and Woodall 1998). They argue that CISD rests on unquestioned assumptions and the practitioners' beliefs, which have become the new paradigm or conventional wisdom. They argue that its practitioners are a 'social movement' whose work is based on poor empirical evidence, and an unsubstantiated idealized view of the personalities of emergency services personnel – such traits as perfectionism, which allegedly make staff more vulnerable to guilt, etc. They take issue particularly with the origins of details of the theory, such as the 'rescue personality' of emergency services personnel. It is a long and detailed article, which deserves to be read by anyone who is interested in CISD – or indeed in post-traumatic stress disorder amongst disaster victims, where there is an overlap between post-traumatic stress and critical-incident stress – although we ourselves think the jury is still out on the subject. The authors bring to bear a combination of academic rigour and scepticism together with practical experience; Woodall, for example, brings fifteen years' experience in the Arizona fire service.

Children may suffer the effects of a disaster, regardless of whether they were directly involved or were witnesses. They can experience effects by dint of having 'nearly' been involved, or by having friends or casual school acquaintances who were involved. The same comment also applies to adults, such as school staff, who were not present at an incident but may feel profoundly affected all the same.

Most workers in our situation spend time reminding adults of the need to be sensitive to children's needs, but some adults may worry about going too far. Adults may equate 'providing support' with 'letting children do what they like'. Teachers or carers may feel uncertain about what to do about a child's behaviour, if the behaviour would normally warrant some kind of discipline or sanction. It is important that the children see the adults around them as 'safe' and dependable, that some parts of life are constant. This is more likely to happen if adults try to respect and maintain normal standards of behaviour, with reminders of reasonable behaviour (importantly) being used in a constructive and positive manner. Feedback must be positive. All that we would ask of adults is that they be willing to provide support, to listen and to respect a child's experience.

Adults should also be prepared for very explicit questions from children. Euphemisms such as a dying person 'going to sleep' may cause confusion about death and night-time. Whilst an adult may prefer to speak about generalities or refer to death in a supernatural way, it is possible that younger children will want to ask questions about injuries or burial.

Just as not all individuals react similarly to a personal bereavement, not all groups of people react similarly after a disaster. Disagreements may arise about what kind of reaction to a tragedy is warranted, and what is 'over the top'. For example, a newspaper journalist took issue with the 'grief police' who allegedly prevented normal life from operating in the first weeks of September 1997, after Diana's death. In reply, the father of a Dunblane victim took issue with the 'anti-grief police', and commented that 'following a tragedy different people react in different ways. Yes it is wrong to insist that everybody grieves, but it is also wrong to insist that nobody grieves, simply because it embarrasses others.' (The article was by Euan Ferguson, *Once More With Feeling*, the Review Section of the *Observer*, Sunday 30 August 1998. The response was in a letter to the *Observer*, Sunday 6 October 1998. The example cited was that of wishing to place a Christmas tree in Dunblane cemetery, and the resistance to this idea by other families.)

Disasters are unique in that the tragedy involves a community-wide body of people (if not literally a 'whole community'), and for a while the dynamics that are set in motion are similar to those visible in embryonic social movements. In the aftermath of a disaster, after the initial shock, there can be a real sense of a community working together, and a sense of comradeship or community spirit. For some people, it is as if something positive is found in the shared experience. It is possible to see expressions of idealism and altruism. As a sense of normality establishes itself and other factors in everyday life re-impose themselves, this community spirit can be diminished as people's attention moves away from the key event and toward other, individual events. The resultant loss of idealism can lead to disillusionment, and despair or anger may then be expressed. Similar experiences were observed in Warrington after the bombings of 1993 – many people wanting to return to normal life after the early shock of the events, and others who (possibly encouraged by news media) maintained the experience and tried to create formalized long-lasting social structures, the 'peace movement'. Older children will certainly be as aware of, and as vulnerable to, these complicated and confusing dynamics as are adults.

Most disasters occur within or to a discrete community which is already recognizable long before the disaster occurs, whether a football club or a school or some other group in which people know each other. Transport disasters are different in that the survivors involved may be strangers to one another, who may go their separate ways after the immediate aftermath, and feel particularly estranged from those around them in their normal lives who have not shared their trauma. If they can be said to belong to a single community at all, it is one that is created by the shared experience of the disaster.

In his paper, 'The Effects of Disasters on Children', Professor Yule commented on the rise of the public awareness of death and bereavement, particularly in the wake of the high-profile disasters of the mid and late 1980s – Piper Alpha, Hillsborough, *Herald of Free Enterprise*, Bradford FC, to name only a few (Yule 1989). Yule highlighted the following points in relation to teenagers who had been involved in transport-related disasters (particularly involving ships and ferries):

Sleep disturbance

Almost all children had major sleep problems in the first few weeks. They reported fears of the dark, fear of being alone, intrusive thoughts when things are quiet, bad dreams, nightmares, waking through the night. Problems persisted over many months. Use of music to divert thoughts helped.

Separation difficulties

Initially, most wanted to be physically close to their surviving parents, often sleeping in the parental bed over the first few weeks. Some distressed parents found their clinging difficult to cope with.

Concentration difficulties

During the day, children had major problems concentrating on schoolwork. When it was silent in the classroom they had intrusive memories of what had happened to them.

Memory problems

They also had problems remembering new material, or even old skills such as reading music.

Intrusive thoughts

All were troubled by repetitive thoughts about the accident. These occurred at any time, although often triggered off by environmental stimuli – e.g. movement on a bus, noise of glass smashing, sound of rushing water, sight of tables laid out like the ship's cafeteria. Thoughts intruded when they were otherwise quiet.

Talking with parents

Many did not want to talk about their feelings with their parents so as not to upset the adults. Thus, parents were often unaware of the details of the children's suffering, although they could see they were in difficulty. There was often a great sense of frustration between parents and children.

Talking with peers

At some points, survivors felt a great need to talk over their experiences with peers. Unfortunately, the timing was often wrong. Peers held back from asking in case they upset the survivor further; the survivor often felt rejected.

Heightened alertness to dangers

Most were wary of all forms of transport – not willing to put their safety into anyone else's hands. They were more aware of other dangers. They were affected by reports of other disasters.

Foreshortened future

Many felt they should live each day to the full and not plan far ahead. They lost trust in long term planning.

Fears

Most had fears of travelling by sea and air. Many had fears of swimming, of the sound of rushing water.

(See also the report of a speech by Professor Yule: Chris Mihill, 'Children hide long term stress to avoid upsetting adults', *Guardian*, 5 April 1993.)

When children have been involved in a disaster, several points will need to be kept in mind by both the family and by professionals who try to help them:

° It is wise to reunite the children with surviving parents and family as soon as practicable in the aftermath of the event.

° Children can regress to an earlier stage of emotional development and behaviour; teenagers may go back to sleeping in the parental bed.

° The survivors may need to talk over what happened so as to get the sequence of events clear in their minds as well as to gain control over the feelings that their memories will generate.

° Repetitive retelling is not enough alone. Professionals can help by creating a relatively safe environment in which such recounting can take place; but bear in mind that it is not helpful to place pressure or a burden onto the children by 'expecting' them to speak out.

° Experiencing that the world does not come to an end when feelings are shared between parent and child can be very facilitating.

° Learning that other survivors share similar, irrational guilt about surviving can help to get things in perspective.

° Learning how to deal with anxiety attacks, how to identify trigger stimuli, how to take each day as it comes – all are important tasks.

Patricia Hagan, a Principal Clinical Psychologist working in Liverpool, submitted a paper called 'Types of intervention following a disaster' to the Department of Health Working Party on the Social and Psychological Consequences of Disaster, in 1990. The following observations are based on her submission, paying particular attention to the school and community based responses and to aspects of community empowerment. The paper as a whole was concerned with strategies to help a community – children and young people are only a part of a community, so these are summaries of the most relevant points in reference to children's needs:

° Proactive initial contacts should be made with all those directly involved, to offer them the opportunity to talk through the experience and their feelings. It is useful to send a letter saying that someone will call on them, giving them a date and time, and ask them to cancel if they do not want to be visited. The initial visit can be used to provide information on the range of normal reactions, an assessment of needs and risk, and to inform family members of where they can go to for help. Calling cards can be left with everyone visited giving the worker's name and the number of the helpline or office.

° Extensive advertising of the helpline and counselling services/centres is necessary. Although support services will inevitably include an element of counselling, survivors or the bereaved may at times simply need company. Or they may need practical help: someone to go with them to visit the scene of the disaster; to help them through official procedures; or to act as an advocate. Group work will very likely be suggested, and be useful. Assistance can range from the bringing together of individuals as a self-help group to leading an intensive analytical therapy group. Following a disaster, group work is likely to fall in the middle of these with people who have shared particular experiences meeting with professional leaders. Again it should be recognized that working with groups, which can generate powerful dynamics, is a skilled activity for which leaders should have appropriate training and understanding so that groups can be properly planned, their aims clearly identified and their processes understood.

° The majority of those affected by the disaster, who do not seek personal counselling, will be most supported by community work. Community work facilitates the process of the community at large coming to terms with what has happened to them, through community meetings and projects to rebuild damaged parts of the community. Support and training can be given to youth workers and teachers to help them facilitate the process of children expressing their feelings about the disaster, and acknowledging their own ways of coping. This may be particularly important in cases where children are reluctant to say anything at home for fear of further distressing their parents, or in cases where the disaster has particularly affected a school community or a youth group.

° A regular newsletter should be sent out to all survivors and those bereaved by the disaster. This gives them a means of contact with each other and is a way to provide information about coming events, meetings and legal proceedings. It is also a place to ask for ideas about memorials and anniversary events. The newsletter can be organized initially by the disaster team and then taken over by a group of those more directly involved. For example, *Interlink* was the Hillsborough newsletter.

CHAPTER 4

Disaster
How Can Schools Respond?
Elizabeth Capewell

° On 21 October 1990, two children and their mother died in a house fire witnessed by many on the surrounding estate. The school became a focal point of help and played the role well during the following year. Teachers were briefed on what to expect. Extra help was brought in and referrals were made where necessary. Memorials and anniversaries were handled sensitively and both teachers and children learned a great deal about death and what to do when people are bereaved. This last response is still rare – change in the way that traumatized children are viewed has been slow. Adults feel challenged by the idea that, in the end, they cannot protect children from horrific reality and untimely death.

° Children involved in Australian bush fires were reported by teachers and parents to have fully recovered from the experience. However, on being assessed eight months later this was found to be far from true.

How are children affected?

Children are no more and no less resilient than adults. Some are more resilient than others. The same child may be resilient to one event but react quite differently to another.

Take yourself back to your childhood and feel again the turmoil of an upsetting event, with the adult world buzzing around above your head, too involved with its own distress to recognize yours. It becomes easier to understand that the reactions of a child to a traumatic event are merely the *normal* reactions of anyone. It is the event which is abnormal, not the child.

Remember too that no one is a blank sheet – previous or present life experiences may compound the trauma. No child should be denied help because they are from a 'problem' family or have a 'neurotic' mother, as sometimes happens.

Some common reactions

Most of these reactions can occur in children of any age, as older children often revert to 'young' behaviours:

- Sleep problems, e.g. nightmares, fear of going to sleep.

- General fear and worries, often through not understanding.

- Overwhelming emotions – tears, sadness, grief, anger (often directed at teachers, parents, friends).

- Inappropriate emotions and reactions, e.g. hysterical laughter.

- Reversion to old toys, comfort objects, bed-wetting.

- Worry and embarrassment about emotions and reactions.

- Clinging – sleeping with parents, not letting go.

- Denial – avoiding issues and places; 'forgetting' or fantasizing.

- Performance decline – lack of concentration and motivation.

- Foreshortened future – refusal to plan ahead.

- Changes in behaviour – aggression, silence, attention-seeking.

- Psychosomatic complaints.

- Lost childhood – 'too old, too fast' even if very young.

- Low self-esteem, shame, guilt, loss of trust in the world.

- Acting rebelliously, substance abuse.

° Eating problems.

° Specific fears triggered by reminders of the trauma.

° Obsessive retelling of events and preoccupation with self.

° Feeling different from friends – they seem flippant/immature.

The role of the school

Education has a major part of play in the response to disaster and the role involves ordinary classroom teachers and situations. Some points to remember are:

1. Children are always affected by disaster, whether directly as survivors, bereaved and witnesses, or indirectly as friends, TV viewers and children of rescuers and other disaster workers.

2. Schools are often directly involved, e.g. in Hungerford, the Towyn floods, school trip incidents and minibus crashes.

3. School is a large part of a child's life. What happens there and what affects it is important to all. The school provides the main support and social network.

4. School is the normal place for a child to be and offers security at a time of insecurity. Trauma reactions are normal reactions and are best helped in a normal environment.

5. Those who do need clinical help still go to school.

6. Children are in school in their own right, not because they have a problem or carry a 'survivor' or 'victim' label. This is important as survivors often feel a loss of power and dignity. Seeing a social worker or psychologist still carries a stigma and at school you have a choice about who you talk to.

7. The way adults respond to children can significantly affect the outcome of their experience; thus the reactions of teachers who they see daily are vital – the teachers need to be informed. Teachers often unwittingly cause more problems for children.

8. Teachers have known the children before the disaster and may see them for several years after. They are in a prime position to observe behaviour changes, delayed shock and reactions which are not being resolved, and can make referrals.

9. Teachers have many skills and techniques which, with a little training and awareness, can be adapted to help children cope with trauma. These can be used in normal class lessons and will reach the many affected children who would not seek other help and those who can give support to their friends.

10. Such crises can provide opportunities for a great deal of real-life learning at a time when children want and need to find solutions. What is education for if it is not about real life?

What schools can do

For schools to respond well to traumatic events, they must have full support from their managers. These events create a considerable emotional and financial burden on schools and other school services which are already overstretched by normal workloads. Time and money invested in emergency planning, training for managers and staff, and wise use of specialist consultants at key points will be repaid by the resulting reduction in costs of supply cover for sick staff and hidden costs of stressed pupils. It is important that schools devise a crisis intervention plan.

Pre-crisis

Few schools and teachers are interested in death and disaster courses or planning – until disaster strikes. Then, they want to know everything in the space of an hour's staff meeting. In an hour it is impossible to give all the answers to the questions of life and death, and to explain exactly what to say and do with each pupil, parent and the media, how to deal with individual staff reactions and previous life traumas, and how to understand the complex dynamics which arise in a stressed staff group, with management, and between different agencies.

Stress prevention and death education is a good preparation for many aspects of life so will not be wasted if disaster does not strike.

This is what I recommend:

1. *Stress prevention and death education programmes.* These can be developed as a natural part of the school curriculum, involving topics such as relaxation techniques, problem-solving, decision-making, communication skills and developing and maintaining support networks. Being at ease with emotions and learning how to give and receive support is also important. A lot of heartache can be reduced if friends know how to help each other and realize that taunts about death of a parent or friend are hurtful. Trauma and death-specific information can be added where appropriate.

2. *Staff training.* Education programmes will not work unless staff are at ease with the subject, can model appropriate ways of dealing with stress and grief, and have had an opportunity to work out their own beliefs and feelings about death and trauma.

   Training which ensures good team relationships, management and communication will provide a solid foundation for dealing with a crisis. And don't forget to train the clerical and auxiliary staff, too – they are vital in an emergency.

3. *School emergency plan.* This should be flexible, accessible, easily understood, and regularly updated. It should include emergency phone numbers, planning checklists, a letter to parents which can be easily adapted to circumstances, and basic information sheets about post-traumatic reactions.

A good administrative system in a crisis saves untold stress, so attend to that, too.

When disaster strikes

Too often, in the panic, solutions are thrown at imagined problems and time and money are wasted. This is where pre-planning counts. Whatever the chaos and state of preparation, three things are essential:

° Planning

° Assessment

° Debriefing.

Each stage may only take a few minutes. Planning may just be jotting down your next three steps; assessment may be a quick head count; and debriefing may be a few minutes to shed some tears or to check with colleagues what each is doing and how you are feeling. Its purpose is to gain a sense of control and stop tension building up.

Post-impact

Pre-planning will ensure that information dissemination and debriefing occur in the first week when it is most effective and there is still time to reduce trauma reactions. A more considered approach is now possible but the three essentials still apply: plan, assess, debrief.

1. *Planning.* Collate information; note what else needs to be known. Decide on the school's role in relation to other agencies. Formulate your action plan within the school, with parents and, if relevant, in the community. Identify resources.

2.   *Information.* The starting point for regaining control is
     knowing the facts, understanding what happened and
     accepting reality. Young children can cope with horrific
     reality if the truth is told simply and directly. Rumours spread
     quickly and can create secondary crises, especially where
     people are being blamed.

     Inform, for example through a leaflet, about sources of
     help and likely reactions.

3.   *Assessment.* Assess the extent of the school's involvement in
     terms of numbers and vulnerability. Do a simple check down
     the register to note who was involved and who is likely to be
     affected, including witnesses, relatives, friends/enemies, and
     those who but for chance could have been there. (The
     number of people affected is usually underestimated.)

     Next, check the register for those who are vulnerable
     because of recent deaths, trauma or general family problems.
     Do the same for staff. More detailed screening of pupils can
     take place later to check assumptions about who is involved
     and affected.

4.   *Debriefing.* This is a structured and very important process
     which allows the initial trauma to be dealt with so that the
     other processes of grieving and healing can begin. In a
     trauma, images are 'burnt' on to the memory and these need
     to be relived, released and reorganized. This is true, too, for
     helpers such as teachers who are shocked by the news and
     then hear countless horrific stories from pupils.

     In working with schools, I have found debriefing to be
     one of the most useful processes. It sorts out the facts,
     squashes the rumours, helps understanding of why certain
     actions were taken, enables an exchange of feelings and ideas,
     and allows time for teaching. For less-serious incidents and
     for those indirectly involved, an informed and trained
     classroom teacher could be able to debrief their pupils.

5.   *Resumption of normal routines.* Normal routines should be resumed as soon as possible. This is not the same as pretending nothing has happened. It allows the crisis-related work and events such as funerals and memorials to be set against the safety of known and predictable routines.

Practical help for classroom work

When a crisis occurs, an opportunity is provided to learn about sensitive issues where everyone is involved in some way (unlike individual bereavement). It provides real-life learning about feelings and relationships and tolerance of different feelings and reactions.

It is not appropriate in this chapter to describe all the creative work that is possible in the classroom. The most important prerequisite is that the teacher has gained, through training, the confidence to adapt his/her normal teaching skills to sensitive situations.

Above all, don't go for the extremes of insensitive dismissal of feelings or over-sensitive protection of children. Allow pupils to tell you what happened in a way which is appropriate for their age and development. Young children will use explicit play about the event quite naturally. Don't stop them but help them work out any problems they can't resolve.

Sort out facts from fiction and create a safe environment for sharing stories and holding structured discussion of reactions. For those who can't or won't talk, don't force them. Suggest others they can talk to, and provide opportunities for free expression through art, clay modelling, stories, drama and poetry.

Give pupils help with writing letters to the injured and bereaved and discuss how they can help friends while absent from school and when they return.

Particularly watch out for irritability, irrational anger and difficult emotions which can be misinterpreted. Teach coping skills and offer information to reassure pupils that these are normal reactions. If necessary, refer them to expert help and repeat information on where to get extra help – distressed people often don't remember what they hear the first time.

Note

This is an edited extract from the author's article in *National Council of Parent–Teacher Associations Newsletter*, March 1992, designed to highlight key practical issues. Readers who are interested in the full document are referred to the original publication. The comments made here are of course applicable to a range of youth/schools type groups.

Since writing this article, Elizabeth Capewell has undertaken further research and reflections on her experience of disaster work in a variety of school contexts, including work related to the Troubles in Ireland. She is Director of the Centre for Educational Responses to Trauma and Stress (CCME).

CHAPTER 5

Using an Educational Model to Foster Children's Resilience in the Context of a Bereavement Service

Ian Morland

The purpose of this chapter is to describe the values and philosophy which were developed through the practice of working with bereaved children. The emphasis will be on promoting a model for practice, describing how and why this model was developed, and then describing how its success can be measured. An outline of the theoretical concepts involved in bereavement and resilience will lead to a description of methodologies for group work, guidelines for what we consider achievable, and general comments on research and evaluation. It is my hope that these theoretical explorations will be valuable to other professionals, and all concerned adults, in their own work with children and young people.

Listening to children

We said earlier that children's voices were not being heard. What do we mean by this?

Children tend to experience either of two extremes as a result of bereavement. On the one hand, they may be excluded from the imminent death and subsequent grieving when somebody dies, whilst adults either try to protect the child or else assume that the child does not or cannot experience the same emotions as adults do. It is quite possibly correct that our society is still carrying Victorian romanticized stereotypes of children and childhood, so that (despite all the evidence and our own early experiences) we tend to expect childhood to be more carefree and happier than it frequently really is (Grollman 1991).

On the other hand, children may find themselves being expected to behave and react in certain ways, and may find that adults decide that they (the children) need counselling – on the basis that the adults' expectations of the children are not being met.

To take an example of the latter. A young girl was distressed at the death of her mother, and disturbed her father by taking her mother's photograph to him during the night. In this example, is the girl's behaviour a sign of unresolved psychological processes, or is the situation basically that the child is looking for reassurance and the father is (quite naturally, in view of his own loss) incapable of providing it?

Or to take another example. A father seeks counselling for his young son, who still grieves for his mother who died two months ago after a long illness. The father has 'dealt with' his grief and doesn't understand why his son is so distressed – but is it the son who is in need of help, or is it the father?

Or to take a third example. A grandmother is distressed and obviously angry at the death of her own adult child, and is now looking after an orphaned grandchild. The grandchild appears to be better able to cope with the situation than the grandmother, and yet the latter seeks help for the former.

With these three examples, it is clear that adults' views toward children can be contrary to our stated aims, and by adopting one extreme or the other we as adults can stifle the authentic voice of the child (see Pithers 1990).

Even caring adults with the most well-meaning of intentions can do and say counter-productive things, either by over-protecting the child or by placing unrealistic expectations on the child. How can we hear what children need if we cannot honestly and openly listen to them?

With the correct kind of approach, and with unforced encouragement, workers will find for themselves that children will begin to relate their own personal stories, either by action or verbally or in writing (Barnard and Kane 1995). By creating a 'safe listening space', it becomes possible to identify the children's own distinct needs for accessible information and advice, advocacy and support. Our own experience showed that in general children, with appropriate knowledge and support, have the capacity to be resilient in the face of sudden unexpected events in their lives; and have the ability to retain their social role, presence and social development.

The social context of bereavement work

Bereavement is an area of practice where the norm is for services to be utilized much more by families from middling and higher socio-economic groups. This is because bereavement work is not a statutory service and is therefore discretionary, and so literacy, language skills and verbal reasoning are often necessary prerequisites for those who wish to gain access to bereavement services. Why are these prerequisites important? It is important here to say a few words about the different approaches to working with bereavement. It is also important to be fair to many bereavement practitioners, by recognizing that their practice and methodologies may be more diverse than their theoretical background may lead us to think.

'Counselling' is a term which is widely used and unfortunately it seems to have become attached to a wide range of uses which reach far beyond the therapeutic – 'counselling' in the work place, as another term for supervision or mentoring, for example. Counselling, at least in the context of bereavement work, is much more closely related to therapy and the therapeutic schools: it is very much a view of the client as somebody who is overwhelmed by grief and appears incapable of adapting to loss, and so the practitioner becomes engaged in exploring the client's personal emotional landscape. Particularly with practitioners who have a background in medicine or psychiatry, it is a relationship which can be very reminiscent of the doctor–patient relationship – even the language borrows from that heritage, with words such as 'therapy', 'treatment' and so on.

In contrast, the work that many practitioners actually do with their clients can be more diverse than this philosophy may lead us to expect – no real-world example is ever as narrow as the stereotype which describes it. For example, Winston's Wish (a child bereavement group based in Gloucestershire) introduced the 'Camp Winston' model, which was borrowed from the distinctly non-therapeutic American Summer Camp children's holiday model; whilst in contrast, some of the work undertaken by Winston's Wish is closer to the traditional model of therapeutic individual work and assessment (Stokes and Crossley 1996).

Or to take the example of Liverpool Children's Project – LCP staff (Gillian Moore and Julie Nagy) would use books as means of engaging with children and their imaginations, whilst in the hands of Grace Zambelli and Arnold DeRosa this same practice becomes 'bibliotherapy' (Zambelli and DeRosa 1992). In this latter example, the linguistic turn gives the game away, that Zambelli and DeRosa are working from a medical therapeutic model, even though they are using a straightforward method of engaging with children.

These two brief examples illustrate that it is very possible for a practitioner to base their work on therapeutic models and see themselves as a part of that tradition, whilst also using non-therapy but more child-friendly and community-friendly methodologies as a part of their work. This is not to criticize those practitioners, but to point out the dangers of stereotyping all therapeutic/ counselling models. It is as if these different practitioners are like a person who is chained to a post in the ground: they can enjoy the benefits of roaming across a given area, but are always tied to that post and cannot move further than the chain permits. The post is the philosophical anchor behind the practitioners' work, and the chain can be either long or short depending on the strength of belief that they carry from their philosophy into their practice.

With the above caveat, we can now examine the methodologies of those therapeutic traditions which do *not* reach out so easily to engage with their clients. Within the wide range of bereavement services commonly available in Britain, some models of work generally display particular factors. These result from the models' structured nature and from their theoretical origins and may be described as follows:

1.   The main medium of communication is verbal.

2.   The focus of communication is the client and/or their personal issues.

3.   There is a counsellor (or more than one) and a client (or more than one), and there are distinct, explicit or implicit roles and expectations for each of these.

4.   The practice is often confined to fairly specific beginning and ending times, which are planned in advance.

It emerges from these points that a 'successful' client for counselling would be: a person who is sufficiently self-aware to begin to recognize their own emotional position; is sufficiently verbally articulate and confident to be able to seek out available services and then discuss their needs with a counsellor or with peers in a formalized setting; and who feels sufficiently at home with this kind of culture. The consequence of this is that those who are less confident verbally, and less able to express their needs through that particular cultural context, have tended not to receive support, or to receive inappropriate support. Access to services is an enduring difficulty for service providers, across a range of subjects beyond bereavement work.

It is still true that some people will not make use of formal counselling services because of their own beliefs and traditions of thought. This is possibly because of a misplaced sense of pride (i.e. that they ought not to need such a service), and a stigma that is still associated with this kind of work. Those readers who are interested may see parallels here with what has been written about 'philanthropic' voluntary organizations in general (Knight 1993, pp.88–97).

On the basis of what young people were actually saying to workers, we learned that a counselling or group therapy methodology ought not to be always the first and most obvious method for meeting young people's needs, despite its usefulness for some people. For example, if children 'often feel awkward and uncomfortable' with a particular technique, as one practitioner reported (Smith and Pennells 1995, p.40), this may indicate that a change in technique is required, rather than attempting to educate the child into the ways of the therapist. The encounter between doctor/therapist and child/client can be the meeting ground of two very different views of the world, and why should we expect children to meet us on our terms? Katon and Kleinman described these kinds of encounters and the differences of interpretation between doctors and patients, and how 'negotiation' was needed to reach a common understanding (Katon and Kleinman 1981).

The importance of cultural factors for good practice needs to be remembered. There are cultural differences between different ethnic communities which have an effect on how people understand and express their experiences; these should be recognized for what they are, and be respected. Equally, there are other innumerable but subtle cultural differences between different social groups and classes, for example the bereavement practitioner and urban primary-school-aged children. It becomes harder to make sense of experiences in isolation from one's own culture; in fact, differences in culture may have a huge impact on permissible ways of expressing feelings.

Poverty and social deprivation are also very important factors in the social context of bereavement. Accessible bereavement services ought to be made available in areas of deprivation, because evidence suggests that needs may be greater there. For example, Winston's Wish in Gloucestershire estimate that in their target population of 500,000 people, there would be 200 children bereaved each year (Stokes and Crossley 1996). We would add that the higher incidence of deprivation and poverty in cities such as Liverpool is likely to have an impact on future coping after the event of a death.

The Department of Health has consistently identified that illness, accident, death and even suicide occur at rates well above the national norms in areas of high deprivation. It cannot be coincidence that three reports over the past eighteen years have highlighted that ill health and mortality go hand-in-hand with poverty: the poorer one is, the more likely one is to become bereaved. The landmark Black Report (Black 1980) was followed in 1987 by Margaret Whitehead's 'The Health Divide', which included the comment that the 'lack of services in high-risk localities can compound the damage done by the environmental factors' (Townsend, Davidson and Whitehead 1992, p.356). The most recent addition to this library is Sir Donald Acheson's 'Inequalities in Health' report of 1998. Acheson observes that 'although the last 20 years have brought a marked increase in prosperity and substantial reductions in mortality to the people of this country as a whole, the gap in health between those at the top and bottom of the social scale has widened' (Acheson 1998, p.v). The Acheson Report goes on to explain a policy position which fits perfectly with our own position regarding bereavement, that is, that a medical model is not adequate for resolving the issues involved. Sir Donald writes that 'the weight of scientific evidence supports a socio-economic explanation of health inequalities. This traces the roots of ill health to such determinants as income, education, and employment as well as to the material environment and lifestyle' (Acheson 1998, p.xi). The difference between bereavement practitioners and a government is that we cannot change the socio-economic circumstances: I shall explain later what we can achieve. The important point is to recognize that it is inadequate to think of bereavement and ill-health as problems of the individual. Individuals do not exist in a vacuum. Of course, the above findings are by no means unique to Britain: in the United States, five per cent of children will lose one or both parents by the age of 15, although 'this percentage is substantially higher in lower socio-economic groups' (Zambelli, Clark and Heegaard 1989, pp.61–62).

The pre-existing or structural economic factors are comp-ounded by the fact that a death in the family can lead to a significant loss of household wealth and income: for example by the death of the main bread-winner, and possibly by the resultant loss of the family's home and neighbourhood as well as 'lifestyle'. What happens if the deceased person had a particular role or task in the child's life – such as taking a child to football games, or being a confidante – and so the child no longer has access to these hitherto taken-for-granted social facilities? Possibly, a child may have to move to a new school as well – with added stresses of having to make new friends. It becomes clear from this that bereavement may be traumatic in more ways than the most obvious ones. The social dimension is of great significance.

It therefore becomes a key question, which type(s) of service are the most likely to reach all those who need assistance? Whilst accepting that there is little that bereavement services can do about poverty and deprivation, what they can do is ensure that children and young people are not disadvantaged or excluded by their service provision. Acheson again suggests that policies likely to have an impact on health should be evaluated in terms of their impact on health inequalities (Acheson 1998, p.xi). In Liverpool, one of many cities where poverty and deprivation are realities, our Project piloted and established a model of work which was accessible to children and families, both geographically and economically, across the city.

Children and children's organizations are also identifying other experiences which require accessible service support. These include issues as diverse as terminal illness (cancer and other illnesses), HIV and AIDS (where either the carers or the children are ill), domestic violence and its impact on the child, the traumas of separation and divorce, and the experiences of war refugees (for example, Liverpool's Somali Community). These questions and issues all present a challenge for service providers. The key is to develop work which owes less to the application of a methodology based on theory, and owes more to a respect for methodologies which are meaningful to service users in their own terms, which they can 'own' (take possession of, and then take control of) for themselves. In this respect a successful service will also be an empowering one.

Theoretical considerations for bereavement working

It is easy to forget that bereavement and mourning are natural phenomena, that people have been dying and have been mourning others for as long as people have existed. Technological approaches have helped us to forget this lesson.

It is argued that some bereavement services may actually create difficulties of their own: John McKnight used a lecture to the Schumacher Society to identify four main problems which are created by professionals' encroachment into community relationships in general, and which are created by bereavement counsellors in particular (McKnight 1984).

The first problem is the financial cost incurred by the training and employment of skilled professionals in the act of providing a bereavement service. If these professionals' skills are not always necessary, then this financial investment is not well spent and could be much better used elsewhere.

The second problem is one of side-effects. We are accustomed to treating side-effects from drug medication, but organizations and institutions can cause comparable social side-effects. Each kind of side-effect requires further interventions to repair the unintended damage. This in turn increases the human and financial strain. Even a bereavement service can produce negative side-effects such as encouraging dependency amongst the clients and the undermining of pre-existing social structures. The problem of side-effects is closely allied with the third problem – the loss of knowledge and wisdom by the community because of the people feeling de-skilled by the presence of professionals. McKnight makes the case that bereavement counsellors have unwittingly contributed to the provision of support being dominated by professionals, and to the resultant cult of the expert. This is achieved by professionals who claim that they have indispensable specialist knowledge, and who therefore undermine the confidence of a community to solve its own problems. At worse, professionals may impose their knowledge on communities rather than listening to what people need and then helping them to find answers for themselves. McKnight uses the striking metaphor of colonists who stake their claim on the land. It is also what the historian Harold Perkin has called 'the condescension of professionalism', which has become ultimately the Achilles' heel of professionals by leading them to lose touch with service users and the public (Perkin 1989). For bereavement work, the result of these processes is that those people who knew the bereaved person feel they do not have the knowledge and skills to help. So, professionals may have contributed to a progressive *lessening* of community-based support. A culture can develop in which people are unable to recognize their own ability to help one another, with a 'let's phone the counsellor' approach to problems.

McKnight argues that, in the dependency culture, people rely on professionals and so stop teaching successive generations in their communities how to deal with life's traumas. He cites the example of breast-feeding and how this was effectively suppressed by the well-meaning efforts of the medical profession and the pharmaceutical industry. Another example exists today in Britain: the British Medical Association estimates that 75 per cent of emergency calls to GPs at night are for non-urgent problems. One of the reasons for this is commonly that the parent(s) of a young child become anxious about symptoms which are not life-threatening because these carers have not been able to learn the practical wisdom about child-care which previous generations possessed. The result is an increased and often unnecessary burden on care services, and in the *British Medical Journal* a survey of night-time calls recently reported that '(T)he general practitioners considered many patient contacts to be fairly trivial. They felt that better information could improve the appropriateness of out of hours contacts ...' (Brogan *et al.* 1998). And so the loss of community knowledge creates greater burdens.

McKnight's fourth problem is the élitist and anti-democratic nature of the relationship between 'clients' and 'practitioners' – and the cult of the expert, in which the professional is judged to 'have the answers'. It must be said that the growing emphasis on participation and consultation by the statutory services is an acknowledgement that this is indeed a real social problem. He cites the example of the hospice movement in the USA. The movement's founders sought to 'detechnologize dying – to wrest death from the hospital and allow a death in the family', yet within two decades the movement came to be based again in hospitals, with financial and legislative support for this and the employment of 'physicians as central "care givers" and as managers' (McKnight 1984, p.13). The family and the community became excluded again.

McKnight presents a partisan, polemical case, which is arguably tainted by an over-romantic view of harmonious communities which are capable of mutual aid and support. However, he is by no means alone in sounding a note of alarm at the encroachment of professionalism. As reported in Chapter 2, Richard Grist and S. Joseph Woodall have claimed that critical incident stress debriefing is a 'social movement' phenomenon (Grist and Woodall 1998). Rodney Lowe, in his history of the British welfare state, identified the fact that professionals form powerful élites, which since 1945 have been able to use their specialist knowledge (and consequent social status) to influence changes in public policy in their own favour and to increase their own employment (Lowe 1993, pp.9–38). Harold Perkin, a historian with a more measured view, has written that professionalism's encroachment '... has been done in all good faith: every profession defines its problems in terms of the solutions it is qualified to offer and the service it believes in.' And, to take the example of the formation of the NHS: 'A health service defined and dominated by treatment specialists was bound to be a sickness-oriented system rather than a programme for positive health' (Perkin 1989, p.348).

In a similar vein, because bereavement has been identified as a 'problem' by counsellors and therapists within the health and social work professions, they inevitably believe that it is a therapy-type psychological problem which requires their specialist skills to aid recovery. Alternative possibilities are rarely considered. But, it is sufficient for sceptical readers to agree with what nursing professionals have written, that 'the fact that only psychiatrists and psychologists are seen in western society as having the skills to deal with bereaved children may also prevent support from being given at home or in school' (Beswick and Bean 1996). Yet it is at home and in school that the most effective help could be given. The process is exacerbated if agencies and professionals relate to the child (or child and immediate family) in isolation from the wider networks of kin and community and culture. It is through those relationships that the child makes sense of his/her world and finds 'meaning'.

In one sense, from a child's point of view, the child is bereaved because the surrounding network of relationships is damaged – i.e. somebody who had a relationship with the child has 'disappeared' from the child's life. The need to understand this situation for oneself is surely a process of discovery and learning, a process in which the child is at the centre and for which only the child can be responsible; which means that the child is an active agent in his/her 'learning' rather than a passive recipient of 'treatment'. Importantly, the process of learning is about developing new understandings and conceptualizations, not merely about learning new facts about death.

The questions of how people really live socially, rather than as isolated units, were asked by Martin Heidegger in *Being And Time* (Heidegger 1927). Heidegger is interesting because of the diversity of his influence; he has had an impact on existentialism and psychoanalysis certainly, but also on social science, cultural anthropology and educational theories. It is these latter legacies that interest us the most. He concentrated on the relationship between the person and the world, focusing on community and human relationships. He restated many of the common-sense observations of living which most philosophers had ignored or overlooked.

Heidegger's basic idea was that 'being' is a process rather than a passive state; it is an activity which takes place in a community, and through which experiences can be encountered. He coined the term '*Dasein*' ('being-there') to describe this whole process. Each of us will directly experience the truth of our situation – therefore, truth and knowledge are specific to the situation, and cannot *fully* be perceived from a distance. Nor can they be given to us by anyone else, no matter how expert they are. As George Steiner recently summed this up:

> Man's being must be a 'being-there' ... All Western metaphysics, whether deliberately or not ... has sought to transpose the essence of man out of daily life. It has posited a pure perceiver ... detached from common experience ... This is why metaphysics has loftily relinquished the study of perception to psychology, the understanding of behaviour to morals or sociology, the analysis of the human condition to the political and historical sciences. Heidegger utterly rejects this process of abstraction and what he regards as the resultant compartmentalisation in man's consideration of man.
>
> *Dasein* is 'to be there' and 'there' is the world; the concrete, literal, actual daily world ... (Steiner 1978, p.81)

Another of Heidegger's arguments was that rational thought was only one of the activities of being – what about instinct, intuition, feelings and the senses? We are not rational beings, but we are beings which use reason. Or, as those who work with bereaved children may remember: 'I am not a grieving child, I am a child who may grieve.' This connects perfectly with the dual process model of bereavement, wherein it has been found that a person does not constantly exhibit the symptoms for prolonged periods – he/she can go about their daily life, apparently coping, and yet still be overcome by emotional turmoil (see Stokes, Wyer and Crossley 1996).

It is a truism that for most of our ordinary, everyday lives we direct our full conscious attention toward things only when something goes wrong, when a particular problem arises. For most of the time, we exist in a state of being which is unquestioning, and we more or less take the world for granted. We do not even direct our attention toward our feelings unless they trouble us. Many a car driver will recall driving along a well-known route, and arriving at the destination to realize that they remember little about the journey. A parallel can be drawn with the situation of a child, and how the experience of bereavement sharply draws their attention to issues of their vulnerability, which would otherwise be overlooked. The bereavement alters the landscape around the child, and alters the sense of self and the sense of meaning that derives from the immediate community.

The 'taking for granted' of the world means that using our critical and analytical faculties is not our most natural state of mind. It is easy to forget just how unusual, if not unprecedented, it is for some people to enter into analytical conversations about their feelings and experiences and the processes through which they act. Contrast this with what was said above regarding therapy-based models of practice. The taking for granted of the world goes hand-in-hand with social culture, the learned habits and traditions of the community in which we live. We rely on the minutiae of these to guide us through daily life, which is why culture, and importantly the *differences* between different cultures, is so important.

An alternative model begins to suggest itself. If we take the earlier statement that knowledge is an aspect of being, and we remember that being is an activity, and that both are centred on experience, then it becomes possible to see that if we provide a forum for new activities and experiences to people, then this can lead to the discovery of new knowledge. The person may learn something new about themselves. Just as the child experiencing bereavement is in the unique position of knowing what it is like to be bereaved as a child, so it is true that they are in the exclusive position of being able to learn what the future may offer them. This is the basis for an educational approach rather than a medical-therapeutic one.

Further to this, Heidegger claimed that we engage with others socially, pushing our way toward the future because of our 'care' or 'concern' for the people around us. So, we move forward because of the social, affiliative experiences and qualities in our being. The tools required to make progress are already within the person. The question is whether those tools are accessible.

So far, the issues presented here point inexorably toward the use of an *educational approach* rather than a traditional therapeutic approach for working with bereaved children. Such an approach is strongly influenced by a phenomenological view of human nature. The starting point is the idea that change (i.e. the child's coping with his/her bereavement and then 'moving on' and accepting the future) is driven by an internal striving for social competence; so the child is an active participant and not a passive recipient of experiences. One of the consequences of this approach is that we begin to recognize and accept that the bereaved child has the capacity to overcome the trauma for themselves. It is a question of identifying why some children fare better than others, and this brings us to the central concept of *resilience*.

Resilience in children

In recent years, attention has been paid to resilience by several authorities. Work has been undertaken by the International Resilience Project, on researching resilience in children who have experienced any of several kinds of traumatic incidents in several countries. The Advisory Committee for the Project included representatives from the Civitan International Research Centre, UNESCO, Pan American Health Organization, WHO, International Children's Centre, International Catholic Child Bureau and the Bernard van Leer Foundation. Findings were published in 1995. The final definition that was agreed was that:

> Resilience is a universal capacity which allows a person, group or community to prevent, minimise or overcome the damaging effects of adversity. (Grotberg 1995, p.7)

Michael Rutter defines resilience as a phenomenon:

> ... shown by the young people who 'do well', in some sense in spite of having experienced a form of 'stress' which in the

population as a whole is known to carry a substantial risk of an adverse outcome. (Rutter 1981)

The presence (and absence) of resilience is therefore associated with the divergent reactions of different children to comparable traumatic experiences. In short, the term refers to the factors which enable a person to cope with their experiences. Rutter notes that experiences in themselves have different effects according to pre-existing support structures, experiences, etc. An early parental death does not automatically lead to adult depression, but does give a threefold increase in the likelihood of depression if another event (e.g. redundancy) occurs in adulthood; i.e. bereavement is a significant multiplier or magnifier.

Resilience is a generic concept, which cannot be pinned down to measurable specifics. It is dependent on the person and on the person's environment and history. In practice, it is noted that survival and coping must be socially acceptable – e.g. drugs or prostitution would not be counted as resilient behaviour but as 'avoidance', a failure to find such an adaptation (Osborn 1993). That is, resilience is a value statement of *how* people cope, as well as stating *that* they cope.

However, resilience does throw light on why the child's normal social support structures are not meeting the child's needs, and urges us to rectify this. For example, a surviving parent's support has a direct impact on the child's coping, and there is the added danger that the bereavement can draw an adult's attention away from other 'normal' aspects of parenting (Altschul 1988). Other pressures may prevent care from being provided also. In this context, it should be obvious why so much attention is given above to the problems of poverty and deprivation. If families and communities are already under stress in their everyday lives, they will be less able to cope with the additional events and traumas of bereavement. Their deprivation is likely to mean they are less resilient. The opposite is true for those who do have reliable social supports, and Acheson notes that 'mutual support within a community can sustain the health of its members in otherwise unfavourable conditions' (Acheson 1998, p.6).

The objective of any bereavement support should be, therefore, to increase the capacity of family, friends and communities to support and enhance children's potential for resilience. This recognizes (a) that children exist within an enduring social network, and (b) that any service can only help the child to cope, it cannot offer a 'cure'. Similarly, the International Resilience Project did not study children in isolation from their settings:

> In promoting resilience, any work with children must similarly be in the contexts of their families, their schools, their communities, and the larger society ... These parents, teachers, communities and societies are essential to promoting resilience in children, so attention is centred on the child, but in his or her setting. (Grotberg 1995, p.9)

Table 5.1 The learning model for resilience (with thanks to Roger Adams)

1. The death is a 'given', i.e. workers cannot try to solve a bereavement; aim to increase resilience	Over-arching concept	This is the outcome
2. So, look at what will increase resilience: • self-esteem • self-efficacy • self-in-situation (localized support)	Problem-solving concept	These are dependent variables
3. Achieve (2) via components of workers' practice, for example: • participation • peer support • behaviour of staff • learning – new understanding rather than new information		These are independent variables

So where does this leave the professional worker and the concerned adults who want to help a child? Bearing in mind that a bereaved child would be better able to cope if various community-based supports were present, it falls to adults to provide what they can. The aim is then to increase a child's resilience by means of certain inputs, as shown in Table 5.1. The table illustrates a process–outcome model, which is based on 'variable analysis'; the idea is that by tweaking the 'independent variables' one can bring about a change in the 'dependent variables', and so achieve the desired 'outcome'.

The factors which contribute to resilience

Different authors have described these factors, although their descriptions commonly refer to the environmental factors surrounding a child and the family – social structures (schooling, religious community, and community relationships) and economic factors (loss of income, poor housing, physical deprivation). They also describe the supporting factors within the family, such as the impact of an impaired ability to provide quality parenting. In this context, 'lack of services in high-risk localities can compound the damage done by the environmental factors' (Whitehead 1992, p.356).

Garmezy and Grotberg each identify three protective factors in resilience (Garmezy 1985; Grotberg 1995). Garmezy lists:

° personality features such as self-esteem;

° family cohesion and the absence of discord;

° the availability of external support.

Grotberg provides three slightly different factors, with the following illustrations:

° **'I am'** or the personality features, e.g. self-esteem
These include, for example: 'I am a person people can like and love, glad to do nice things for others, respectful of self and others, willing to be responsible for what I do, confident things will be all right.'

° **'I have'** or the family and external support structures
These include, for example: '... people around me I trust, who love me, people who show me how to do things right and set examples, who set limits for me to help me avoid

danger, who want me to learn to do things myself, who help me when I am sick or in danger.'

○ **'I can'** or the child's own social and interpersonal skills, i.e. the child's tools for learning, doing, making relationships, etc. These include, for example: '... talk to others about frightening things, find ways to solve problems, control myself when angry or upset, see when it's a good time to talk to somebody, and find somebody to help if I need it.'

Importantly, of these factors, Grotberg argues that:

○ **I am** factors can be strengthened by supports but cannot be created.

○ **I have** factors can be both provided and strengthened.

○ **I can** factors must be learned, and can be taught.

Grotberg's list is thus more comprehensive and regards the child as an active participant (**I can** ...). In Grotberg's model, a child would require more than one factor to be present but could cope without possessing all three. So resilience is a result of a complex interplay between the child and the environment. From these factors, it can be seen that resilience is most likely to be consistently improved by the actions of those who are members of the child's community and networks – note that it is teachers, parents, etc. who can ideally do most to help. They can provide local and family support for a child; to strengthen **I have** and **I can** factors.

Michael Rutter (1987) uses terms of 'protective processes' which counter risk and aid adaptation, to assist resilience. He identifies:

○ reduction of risk impact (the personal impact and effects which arise from events, threats and risks);

○ reduction of 'negative chain events' (reducing the breakdown of communication, personal isolation);

○ establishment and maintenance of self-esteem;

○ opening up of opportunities (i.e. providing opportunities to learn, participate, regain control).

It is our argument that Rutter's four processes can be allied with the **I am**, **I have** and **I can** factors of resilience to develop a realistic model for increasing a child's resilience, as will be explained below.

An achievable methodology: use of support groups

Because of the attempt to provide a service in a near-to-normal context, the basis for a support service ought to be a support group. Pearson (1983) defines these as having the aim of offering surrogate systems of help when assistance within the family and community is not available. One of the common factors in different support groups is that *peer support* is available in one form or another. This plays a factor in rebuilding personal confidence.

Pearson suggests that children's groups be formed on the same basis as adult support groups. His proposals go a significant distance toward meeting with the observations made by McKnight about the undermining of community-based support by professionals' support, because the peer support makes the groups more democratic and they are 'owned' by their members. *Participation* can be enhanced by a 'step on, step off' methodology which permits children to come to one group meeting and not the next, therefore not obliging children to either subscribe to a whole programme or prematurely leaving. This was one idea which was used successfully in Liverpool.

The *behaviour of support staff* is important in ensuring that the principles of participation and choice are translated into real action and opportunity; there must be consistency between ideals and actions. This requires the planning of work, and supervision of workers.

In practice, it is likely that even with minimal advertising and promotion, a steady and increasing number of referrals will be made to the group's facilitators. This is partly due to the pressure which modern health and social services are under to find 'specialist' workers who can alleviate some of their casework. It is also, however, due to real and unmet needs in the communities being served. Group facilitators will need to make use of assessment methods to determine whether and when children should join a group – these methods ought to permit self-assessment by the child, again so that participation and building of self-esteem are at the centre of workers' activities.

Zambelli and DeRosa (1992) found that support groups typically are for children who have lost a parent, although this seems to be the decision made by group facilitators; there is no reason why other bereavements should be excluded. They also argue that support groups must differ from psychotherapy models – and should not claim to ameliorate any interpsychic/interpersonal difficulties, which we would agree with.

How a support group increases children's resilience

In this section we shall suggest how those people who know a bereaved child can help to provide Rutter's protective processes, to help strengthen Grotberg's resilience factors. These comments should apply to children's support groups, but can also be of help to adults who are supporting children in the school and in the home. Many of the threads of the earlier sections can be brought together here: it is possible to design a range of activities so as to manipulate and stimulate the components of resilience. Such a range of activities then becomes a vital tool for the child in learning how to cope with bereavement. Activity can and should be fun. It can provide a safe focus to allow gentle explorations of difficult issues. It can strengthen social skills and provide companionship. But, it can also be a valuable educational process in its own right, which allows children to reflect on and change their self-image and assumptions, assumptions which go to the core of the child's difficulties in coping with bereavement. The reader should remember that learning processes include much more than the learning of concrete pieces of information – they can include the learning of new attitudes and ideas. Therefore, group tasks, problem-solving and experiential learning can be combined into a programme, as educational methods that assist the child.

Reduction of risk impact is a part of the 'I have safe supporting structures'

These factors are assisted by children being able to discuss issues within a group in a safe and supportive context. Such supporting structures should avoid the children being overwhelmed by emotions. When the feelings of bereavement are recognized as being common to others who have experienced similar situations, this helps the children to recognize that they are in fact 'normal' people.

The workers should try to maintain the air of normality by entering into the social situations of the children, rather than the children being expected to enter into a different (adult) environment with different formal kinds of behaviour and 'grown-up' or medical/clinical language. For example, where will the adults and children meet, what will they do, how will they sit or speak to each other ... how 'normal' will the event be? Language and explanations must be presented in ways that are understandable, e.g. the use of accessible pictures, graphics, etc. as tools for communication.

It is suggested that for children, art and play reduce tension by redirecting energies from powerful emotions and into the game in hand, and that this enables children to consider the death without being overwhelmed by emotions (Zambelli and DeRosa 1992). It certainly dovetails with many children's preferences for action over words. Short- to medium-term groups can permit the use of art, game-playing, stories, role-play, discussion, etc.

Avoidance of negative chain events strengthen the 'I have a supportive environment' and adds to the 'I am able to trust and rely on others'

Adults in a family whose own grief prevents them from offering traditional parental support and help can perpetuate 'negative chain events' through the family's internal relationships. Within the support group, the workers provide an anchor – socializing with the children yet not being personally overcome by the powerful emotions which can be touched when memories are expressed. It is important that the adults who try to help the children are able to acknowledge their own feelings towards the subject of death and bereavement honestly – has an adult led a 'lucky life' or do they flinch because of painful memories from their own childhood? Personal emotions cannot be ignored, but adults need to be aware of how these influence their ability to help the children.

Within the group, children learn to use other children for comparisons of their own ideas. Peer group support includes greater reciprocity than does the parent–child relationship; there may be greater intimacy, trust, and interdependence. Yule identified, for example, that children would protect their family and parents from further pain by not speaking with them, even though they may speak with their peers (Mihill 1993).

Increase in self-esteem contributes significantly to the 'I am worth knowing, caring about, etc.'

Self-esteem refers to the feelings of worth as a person; self-efficacy refers to the ability to cope successfully with life's challenges. Support groups can bolster a low self-esteem which is caused by bereavement. Self-worth is bolstered by showing how others are coping with similar situations (Osterweis 1984). That is, the social factor is important in order for children to mutually build their own esteem.

Participation is another important factor, in that it provides opportunities for self-efficacy (ability to cope) but also boosts self-esteem. Participation teaches the child that they are worth listening to and are worth being consulted. Not being allowed to participate, or feeling that one is being belittled in some way, will obviously have the opposite effect and undermine the child's ability to cope. It is thus important for participation to be a central part of the process: beginning with initial staff contact with the child and family (asking the child what they think their needs are, do they want to come to a support group, do they have other ideas?), and offering the choice to be involved with each individual group meeting or activity. What activities would they like to do? How? When? Where is available? A whole range of learning opportunities can be opened up here.

Increasing self-efficacy contributes to the 'I can achieve more than I thought I could.'

Children's self-efficacy also increases as they learn to help others; children can feel satisfaction when they complete an art project, or succeed in a task, or become more socially competent through play. It is thus important to give children opportunities to accept safe challenges, ones which are 'risky' yet achievable and realistic (so as to avoid feelings of failure). Children can take risks and learn what they can do, to gain a sense of achievement and thus to raise their self-esteem and to learn something new about themselves and their capabilities. This is at the core of the educational approach to working with bereavement; it is positive and forward-looking rather than placing attention on the child's bereavement.

Opening up opportunities contributes to the 'I can cope …'

Education about death removes the scope for harmful fantasies, and also permits new ideas and understandings to arise. For a child, this will often mean wanting to find out the facts about how somebody died, what happened to them, etc., so the adults need to be prepared mentally and emotionally. The questioning and answering of learning also add to the children's ability to express themselves and to become socially competent in handling their feelings.

The regaining of a sense of their own self-esteem and self-confidence connects with the process of enabling the child to find other community groups, activities such as sports clubs, etc. These other activities will permit the child to return fully to his/her community network and permit any specific group-work service to be withdrawn at a future date.

With an educational approach, the strategies for assisting the children will focus on stimulating their motivation toward social competence, by learning from their own experiences, and by 'problem'-based learning in accepting new challenges. Small group interactive learning fits well into this approach, and so again we have a rationale for fun but challenging activities.

In summary of many of the above ideas, it would be ideal to offer to those children whose essential social networks are no longer available (remembering that 'lack of support = lower resilience') the opportunity to participate in a programme of planned activities and events in groups with other children who have had similar experiences.

It is important to encourage children to become involved in contributing ideas and activities to the work, by means of seeking written feedback, and oral feedback, and to plan future work and events with children participating. Provision of a regular forum through which the children can contribute ideas, information and questions is invaluable.

As was pointed out at the beginning of this section, the focus of the practice should be to employ a structured programme of activities which follow known educational principles; learning is achieved through participation in peer group activities which enhance *self-esteem, self-efficacy* and *social support* (Zambelli and DeRosa 1992; Rutter 1987; Pearson 1983).

Typical activities used by LCP included events such as memory work by use of scrapbooks, video work, adventure weekends, etc. The Hillsborough Project famously met Freddie the Dolphin in the North Sea, in a joint venture with Val Owen of the Alder Centre – a learning opportunity that gave the teenagers involved new horizons (Martin 1992). To illustrate the consistency of these principles as they were applied by workers in Liverpool, it is worth quoting briefly from 'Beginnings', a paper written by Amanda Martin at Liverpool Children's Project in 1993. This may illustrate how these themes were brought together in group work by the medium of using child-friendly activities:

> ... we have set out to give children a voice, in informal settings, involving activities and fun. The significance of the 'fun' is often misunderstood. Bereaved children lose their self-esteem and

self-confidence … Re-building these is part of helping the child to cope and to move on; helping him or her not to get stuck. Fun (play) involves going slightly outside the normal setting (especially in terms of a bereaved home-setting), it involves a taste of adventure, the spice of slight risk, the possibility of the unexpected, the sound of laughter, shouting, the release of energy, open space, plenty of time, the tiredness after a good day out. Each time children take part in a fun activity, they regain a little of their sense of worth, self-confidence, resilience. Exposure to good and happy events and activities counter-acts the weight of the frightening or sad elements of bad experiences. It does not deny them. In the USA much work has been done, within the Catholic Church Social Services in New York and elsewhere, on providing positive, healthy experiences to encourage healthy grieving and restore resilience within a child.

Within these developments it is essential to remember that bereaved children are children first and bereaved people secondly. For example, a child will pass through the normal phases of child development and understanding, and so as a child grows older he/she may come back to the adults with new and challenging questions about a previous bereavement. This does not mean there is a 'problem', just that the child is developing mentally and has found new questions.

Research and evaluation

According to the Central Council for Education and Training in Social Work, in Britain, action research is concerned with the problems of how to take an ongoing, continuing process and to find out whether and how it is working, and how it ought to be modified (Stock, Whitaker and Archer 1989). Action research permits use of evaluation by 'open enquiry': typical questions will be akin to 'Is our service working? In what ways? How can we do more of what we're doing correctly?' The development of any ongoing social work or community work practice will be greatly aided by a commitment to action research, by learning from experiences with children and young people. By focusing on these and similar learning methodologies, adults can safely employ a model of action which will be developmental, i.e. the practice itself will improve and may lead to new discoveries. One is more likely to examine one's own practice and assumptions by this approach, and will be able to examine new aims and goals.

In contrast, many of the methods of evaluation currently used have more in common with 'audit review', an approach which takes for granted the aims and the methods which will be used, and asks relatively 'closed' questions to assess how far through the procedure one has travelled. 'Have we done what we set out to do?' is the kind of question asked here, and is broken down into fine detail. It is a useful method because it is systematic, and it cannot be rejected altogether, but gives no real scope for services to evolve and to shape themselves around service users (Wadsworth 1991).

Warnings should be given, though, for those who are interested in setting up and trying to seriously evaluate their own long-term bereavement support service. For example, when working with children, and especially young children, there is the problem that they cannot answer questions that they do not really understand. This means that the collection of data for research and evaluation purposes is far more difficult than with, say, adults. Care needs to be taken in deciding what the aims of a particular methodology are – for example, improved health, altered behaviour, greater understanding, emotional resilience, etc. There then arises the question of how to measure each of these factors, if indeed they are measurable. What is meant by 'improvement' – removal of symptoms or adaptation to loss? What period of time is required for improvements – one year or ten? On top of all these complications, there is the fact that undertaking research or a social investigation can easily have an impact on the people who are the research subjects, by making those people feel that they are worth studying. So, research is not a neutral activity. The landmark Hawthorne experiments in the USA in the 1930s led to this conclusion and had an impact on business management theory (Mullins 1993, pp.45–48). Practitioners may choose to incorporate some research activity into their work with children with the deliberate aim of benefiting the children. For example, the 'What Helped Me' leaflet (Chapter 8) was a piece of research undertaken to discover what did help a group of bereaved children, but in the knowledge that the process of creating the leaflet may be of benefit to the participants.

What do other bereavement professionals say? There is something of a gap between the academic rigour of social scientists and the practical knowledge of practitioners. Zambelli and DeRosa (1992) describe the prevailing reports of bereavement group work as anecdotal and impressionistic. The inference is that they would prefer more rigorously scientific evaluations, and they comment that those who run children's groups are not skilled in research and resist scrutiny by 'professional evaluators'. The authors overlook the possibility that this is because practitioners distrust the methodologies of the researchers, rather than fearing what may be revealed by research. The difficulties of experimental research are examined by Winston's Wish, with the comment not to suppose that 'just because a research design may conform to a favoured paradigm, then any results will form "reliable knowledge"' (Stokes *et al.* 1996, p.18). To take a look at the 'achievable outcomes' which are outlined here (see below), it is clear that self-esteem and self-efficacy are qualitative rather than quantitative outcomes – they can be evaluated, but not measured in any narrow numerical sense. Yet this does not mean that they are 'anecdotal' or 'impressionistic' – so long as the evidence gained is not utilized uncritically, but is systematically examined in reference to the theoretical model used and in the light of alternative explanations (e.g. Has an improvement occurred? If so, what caused it?) and the research methodology itself is open to scrutiny (Green and Britten 1998). An anecdote may be regarded as a story which has a purpose related to rhetoric or a sense of drama, rather than to inform. As Green and Britten have argued, 'the value of qualitative methods lies in their ability to pursue systematically the kinds of research questions that are not easily answerable to experimental methods', and they are particularly useful for answering different and more difficult kinds of questions. For these reasons, those seeking to assess work with children should not feel compelled to restrict themselves to using limited research and evaluation tools. A practitioner's personal experience is often characterized as being anecdotal, not able to produce general principles which can be widely applied, and a poor basis for making clinical decisions. Yet clinical experience, based on personal observation, reflection, and judgement, is also needed to translate scientific results into treatment of individual patients (Friedson 1970).

Beswick and Bean (1996) wrote that 'Empirical research in this field' (i.e. child bereavement) 'is hampered by the number of direct and indirect variables.' It is true that this is a very complicated area of work. It is also true that patterns of cause and effect, of direct and indirect variables, are confused because they are interchangeable. Clinicians especially need to ask themselves what they are measuring and why, and whether it tells them anything really useful. As Beswick and Bean added, the B/G-Steem self-assessment tool indicated that children in their group had 'a normal level of self-esteem' whilst the workers' experience and observations led them to a different conclusion. It would be risky to rely too heavily on the diagnostic techniques.

It is also important, as we hope this chapter has indicated, not to jump to conclusions but to listen to what children have to say about their needs. It is risky (although common) to make assumptions, such as, 'Counselling after bereavement is one of the few preventative interventions shown to promote mental health in adults, and despite the paucity of good controlled trials there is no reason to believe that it is any less effective in children' (Black 1996). This may be a fair hypothesis which deserves to be investigated, but cannot be used by others as an unquestioned justification for a methodology.

So what can be achieved?

It must be re-emphasized that we are advocating an educational approach to childhood bereavement rather than the more usual counselling/therapeutic approach. This affects the types of outcomes that can be achieved. Key outcomes, which will be real and measurable, include the following:

- ° A child's self-efficacy will increase, when the child is observed to have achieved a capacity to explain their personal experience, for example when amongst members of their community or family, and to interpret the understandings of others (e.g. other bereaved children) as relevant to their own experience of loss. An increase in self-efficacy will also be obvious when the child is observed to be able to make well-informed decisions that will improve his/her future social relationships.

- ° Children's self-esteem will increase, when children are able to use (to their own satisfaction) what may be provided for them as expressive media (e.g. video, music, drama, poetry). These media may be used to communicate the details of the event, and to communicate the impact on themselves of the thoughts, feelings, actions and emotions that are the component parts of their experiences. Self-esteem will also have increased when the child is observed to be able to safely explore social and physical risks, in new situations which were previously perceived to be threatening and to be avoided.

- ° An increase in self-support will have been achieved, when the child is observed to have a successful presence in his/her own community, through stable contacts with children and adults, and will therefore succeed in creating a satisfying social life.

In the long term, evidence will be that the experience of bereavement no longer leads to increased likelihood of referrals for depression and other clinical disorders in adulthood. As Rutter identified (above), good practice can be 'preventative' in that early assistance can help to prevent emotional and psychological problems developing later in life; thus childhood bereavement work can be an economic as well as a humane social investment.

In addition to the above achievements, it is our argument that a bereavement service which is modelled on these lines can meet

McKnight's four specific criticisms (of the professionalization of bereavement services) in the following ways. First, such a service can be cost-effective because it does not distract highly paid and expensively trained physicians, psychologists, etc. from their essential core duties. It is also cost-effective in terms of the avoided treatment costs for adult mental distress (Rutter 1981). Second, being a 'low-technology' type of intervention, it does no or minimal damage to existing social and cultural relationships. Third, it aims to safeguard the knowledge and skills held by the local community and to help families and communities to help themselves. Fourth, it is not predicated on the need to create a professional élite (be they 'bereavement counsellors' or any other specialism) to provide and facilitate this kind of service.

Conclusion

This chapter has demonstrated (a) that there is an increased likelihood of bereavement for those children in lower socio-economic groups, and (b) that these children are likely to be less resilient to trauma than children on average. It is therefore true that bereavement is not simply a matter of personal grief, a psychological problem which can be addressed with psychological solutions; bereavement has a social context. Bereavement services and other professionals are also a part of this social context, and need to respect the implications of their role in society. This chapter has demonstrated that a bereavement service can be developed, whether on formal lines or as part of a community initiative, which uses participation and empowerment with educational principles to help support those children and increase their resilience. It has also suggested ways that a support service can strive to make itself accessible and understandable to children and young people in their own terms. This is not *the* way to run a bereavement support service, but it is *a* way that succeeded. Similarly, I will repeat that we are not suggesting that therapy-based models ought not to be used – we are suggesting that they should be used sparingly and as one tool amongst the many tools which can be used. Zambelli and DeRosa (1992) comment that, 'If support groups are to be considered a viable form of intervention for children, it is necessary to construct a comprehensive theory that describes why and how they work.' We hope that this chapter has done that much at least.

CHAPTER 6

'Human Nature', Social Theory and Methodology

Ian Morland

This chapter describes briefly some of the different approaches used for bringing about improvements in human behaviour. These all contain assumptions about human nature which underlie their methodologies. The history of these theories is an interesting one – many originate in psychology and social psychology but were developed and adapted for use in management theory for business. Only in more recent years, with the introduction of management theories into the public sector, have they been used to encourage many professionals to reflect on their own assumptions and practice. Whilst we advocate an educational approach, other carers may find something valuable here for their own work.

Educational approaches

Educational approaches are strongly influenced by a phenomen-ological view of human personality (Pervin 1970). They assume that human development is driven by an innate, internal striving for social competence. A methodology which draws from this philosophy will concentrate on encouraging and stimulating this motivation. It may include opportunities to learn from one's own experiences, or learn by solving problems or the completion of achievable challenges. Interactive learning in small groups, in particular, where participants have the feeling that they 'own' the activities, fits well into such a theory. The strength of educational approaches lies in linking activities, which aim to induce improvements, to the actual problems and experiences of group members.

Social interaction approaches

Social interaction approaches emphasize that changes in behaviour or attitudes or beliefs are achieved through the interaction with and influence of 'significant other' people (Rogers 1983; Bandura 1986). The strategies which fit well into this approach can be used particularly in the wake of a disaster or a critical incident, when it is important to take the initiative and implement and co-ordinate actions – for example, making use of leaders of opinion to spread information and ideas in the community, outreach visits or facilitation work by respected peers who inform or support others, peer review and support in small local groups, and public pressure to make use of available services.

The value of these approaches lie in their emphasis on communication: that people constantly look to each other for support, approval, role models, information and reassurance.

Behavioural approaches

Behavioural approaches are based on conditioning and controlling behaviour. Pavlov's experiments with dogs are the most familiar example. This is a very mechanistic view of behaviour, drawing on the principles of cause and effect. Human behaviour is seen as primarily influenced by external stimuli, before or after a specific action. The main strategies fitting into these approaches are the reviewing of performance and providing of feedback, giving reminders or signals to reinforce behaviour, and providing incentives or sanctions related to specific actions (rewards, in our context).

Marketing approaches

Other approaches may be useful for explaining how group work or other child-friendly activities can be made attractive to children who may initially be quite wary of trusting whatever is being offered to them. For example, marketing approaches emphasize developing and marketing an attractive product or message that meets the needs of the target group and helps them to achieve their goals (Kotler and Roberto 1989; Rogers 1983).

The message needs to be spread through a variety of channels: mass media such as newspapers, local radio and regional TV, bill boards; on a personal level, through networks of professionals, and using opinion leaders and key people in the community. The effectiveness of marketing approaches may be doubted, although of course the business community has long demonstrated that *not* to take marketing seriously is commercial suicide. Marketing strategies' strengths lie in emphasizing the need to adapt service provision, its style and content, to the target group of service users and carers, with their own particular needs and in acknowledgement of any cultural barriers and taboos. In this respect, the use of marketing strategies may be very helpful to the adults and professionals because of the outward focus of marketing toward the service users (or 'clients', or 'customers'). Marketing helps us to remember that we have to listen to and inform the service users, and enable them to *want* to use the service, rather than relying on our own self-confidence in how important and necessary our services and our knowledge are.

Epidemiological approaches

One other type of approach is useful for its suggestions as to why certain kinds of evidence are valued over others. This is of course important when a network of carers or full-time service providers are asked to justify the continuing investment in provision of support. Epidemiological approaches see humans as rational beings that make decisions on the basis of balancing rational arguments. In theory, if professionals or managers do not take research findings into account then they probably lack convincing information on good care.

The main strategies in these approaches are to summarize the scientific literature and to develop evidence-based guidelines.

Credibility is important: the evidence is expected to be reliable, the guidelines valid, the procedure for developing the guidelines explicit and rigorous, and the organization which sets the guidelines should be credible (Field and Lohr 1992; Grimshaw *et al.* 1995).

The value of these approaches is in their emphasis on a sound proposal for change as well as in summarizing the available evidence. The drawback is that emphasis is inevitably placed on research that delivers the most easily measurable findings, rather than complex in-depth studies which may be more realistic but less conclusive (Haines and Jones 1994). This is the source of much debate in the National Health Service, with the introduction of evidence-based medicine in the search for value for money.

CHAPTER 7

Planning Programmes of Work with Children

Julie Nagy with Roger Adams

This chapter contains examples of how just four different pieces of work can be planned, using a model which specifies the person responsible for managing the process, the purpose and intended result of the process, the people involved in the process, what the piece of work is and examples of the materials which are used to complete it. The table format helps to concentrate workers' attention on the key issues involved.

Table 7.1 Production of the children's 'What Helped Me' leaflet 1994/95

Person responsible	Children, practitioner, TCS graphic designer
Group membership	Children aged 6–12 years who have experienced the death of someone important to them, and who have been involved with LCP over a period of time
Activity	To produce information for the use of other children, and adults, based on the experience of group members
Materials used	Drawing and writing materials, printing contractor
Organization for activity	Individual 1-to-1, and group working
Frequency/ duration	Approx. 6–8 months to research and produce
Progress	• Enable children to produce/design a leaflet which tells their stories through words and pictures, that may appropriately inform other bereaved children • Enable adults to understand child's needs • Enable other bereaved children to find (and be given) community/family-based support for their needs

Table 7.2 Use of video media with children

Person responsible	Practitioner
Group membership	Children aged 6–12 years who have experienced the death of someone important to them
Activity	Children involved in group work, using creative expression to understand the meaning of how death has changed their everyday lives
Materials used	Video camera, paper, pens, location
Organization for activity	Children who have chosen to attend group will work together in decision-making process regarding content
Frequency/ duration	Three sessions
Progress	• Work in group to express thoughts and feelings about loss, to produce stories which translate their experiences • Encounter new experiences and discover new capabilities in themselves

Table 7.3 Use of scrap books	
Person responsible	Practitioner
Group membership	Children aged 6–12 years who have experienced the death of someone important to them
Activity	Children to engage in personal response to death and what is important to them for remembering
Materials used	Scrap books, pens, paper, photographs, stories, music, etc.
Organization for activity	Individual
Frequency/ duration	Monthly
Progress	Build up memory store and share feelings of death with other children and adults

Table 7.4 Evaluation visits to child's home

Person responsible	Practitioner
Group membership	(Individual) children aged 6–12 years, who have experienced the death of someone important to them
Activity	One-to-one home visit, enabling the child to evaluate and speak about their experience of the group
Materials used	Recorded observation
Organization for activity	Meeting at the child's family home (where possible) without carers present
Frequency/ duration	Beginning of programme of activities, in middle and at end; and if the child does not attend two or more activities
Progress	• Ownership of task • Learn about own response and feelings to death, by listening to children and adults, and questioning their own involvement in the group, their progress and knowledge and understanding • Make decisions about their own future

CHAPTER 8

The 'What Helped Me' Leaflet

Claire, Anne-Marie, Angela, Brian,
Michael and Natasha

This is an extract from the leaflet, 'What Helped Me', produced by Liverpool Children's Project. These are the authentic voices of children who had been bereaved, and the articulation of their needs and feelings should speak for itself, both to other children and to their carers and to professionals.

... Put together with the help of Claire, Anne-Marie, Angela, Brian, Michael and Natasha, who have shared their experiences of bereavement so that other children know they are not alone in their feelings following the death of  someone they love. We cannot promise any magic answers to you – all we can do is let you know what helped us ...

◊ It's best to be involved in and given choices about how you say goodbye. It lets you know she's gone.

◊ It can be hard to tell others, but not all people, depends if you trust them or not.

◊ Before the funeral I was allowed to go with my mum and dad to choose a dress for her to be buried in. With her being in hospital a lot this was the first item of clothing we had bought her. It was a pink dress. She lay in the coffin looking so tranquil and restful. As if there was nothing else that mattered. One thing we asked was that nobody, unless they really wanted to, wore black for the funeral. I read at that service and for quite some time afterwards reading on the altar was difficult. Our church was packed with hundreds of people, all whose hearts Natalie had touched.

◊ Sometimes, but not all the time, people feel uncomfortable talking to you.

◊ It's good to spend time with others who've also experienced the death of someone. You may feel lots of different emotions when someone dies like angry or sad, lost or numb.

◊ If you have to move then it's best to be asked where you want to live and who with.

◊ I'm really pleased my parents told me everything that was happening. I think that helped me to handle it.

◊ You should be told all the information if people are ill and are going to die.

◊ It's nice to be able to keep something special that belonged to the dead person.

◊ I coped when my mum and dad died by talking about it, going out with the Children's Project, and days out. I bottled it all up inside and have now learned that it helps to cry. Something else I did that helped was to go to my mum's funeral.

◊ Christmas and birthdays can be sad times.

◊ It helps to talk about things. It makes me feel better.

◊ Sometimes it's good to let your emotions out. It's OK to cry and be angry.

◊ It's not nice if people are pitying you – feeling weird makes me cry.

◊ I still think about Natalie all the time and I miss her a lot.

◊ It helps to remember the good times.

◊ You don't have to be sad all the time.

CHAPTER 9

Summary
Guidelines for Good Practice

° Children have a predisposition toward learning, to make sense of their situation. This can be used to help them.

° Bereavement and death are natural phenomena. So these are not the problem – impaired resilience, confidence and self-esteem are the problem.

° It is not our claim that every bereaved child is in need of a bereavement service.

° Weak or damaged support structures in the child's family or community can increase the need for support from a bereavement service.

° The objective is to enable the child to work upon his/her own challenge to cope with and respond to their trauma.

° A child within a bereavement group does not have to talk about feelings and memories; and if they want to talk then they may prefer to talk with other children, away from adults, or with people not connected with the group.

° A key principle is that a bereavement and trauma service should be *accessible* to those children who need it. It should be understandable in the child's own terms.

° Children should be able to perceive of themselves that they can learn, through *participation* in peer group activities, to make sense of the experience of the bereavement/loss in their lives.

° As much *choice and control* as practicable is to be placed with the child, and the support service should develop via action learning to increase this.

° The service will operate in such as way as to aid the development of *resilience* in the child.

Five Stages of Grief

It is often found helpful to classify the changing reactions to bereavement according to a series of stages, although these ought not to be taken too literally. The grieving process is no mechanical, clockwork operation, although a bereaved person will almost certainly move forward and backward between these five general phases:

1. *Denial*

   Restlessness, being overactive, alternating with apathy. Numbness. Disbelief. Searching for the lost person. Seeing the lost person. Sleeplessness. Loss of sense of identity. Loss of appetite. Disorientation in time and place. Aimlessness.

2. *Anger/guilt*

   Recriminations. Fantasies of violence and retaliation against others. Self-doubt, blaming self and others. Irritability. Anger and fury. Feeling worthless. Swift mood swings between love and hate. Cannot hold onto happy/good feelings. Vomiting, diarrhoea or constipation.

3. *Depression*

   Feelings of abandonment, bitterness, exhaustion. Loss of senses – colour, smell, taste, sound and touch. Loss of interest in caring for self, e.g. washing, eating. Feeling cold. Feeling of experiencing childhood. Weeping, helplessness. Poor judgement of distance and speed. Not seeing to important matters. Poor general health. Psychosomatic illnesses. Severe loss of confidence. Accident prone. Troubled dreams.

4. *Reconciliation*

   Return of energy. Become aware of world outside self. Senses return (smell, sight, sound, taste, touch). Occasional days when thread of life is picked up again. The deceased is seen realistically, i.e. good and bad things are remembered. Warmth and gratitude to carers and supporters. Able to laugh, sense of

humour. Able to appreciate the sun, nature, etc. Still moments of
sorrow and insecurity.

5. *Re-attachment*
    Awareness of others and sense of identity. Warm feelings in
    response to affection and kindness. Coming back to life, to true
    self. Able to travel, go shopping, work. Self-confidence increases,
    able to join in groups. Growing ability to trust, more energy, able
    to take responsibility.

Useful Organizations

Alder Centre

Eaton Road
Liverpool L12 2AP
0151 228 4811.
Helpline: 0151 228 9759
Child death helpline: 0800 282986

Counselling and support for adults, regarding death of a child. Siblings group available for teenagers.

Barnados's Future Matters

Merseyside House
9 South John Street
Liverpool
L1 8BN
0151 708 7848

Working with children/families after diagnosis and before and after death.

Centre for Educational Responses to Trauma and Stress

Roselyn House
93 Old Newton Road
Newbury
Berkshire RG14 7DE
01635 30644
e-mail: capewell@which.not

Compassionate Friends

53 North Street
Bristol BS53 1EN
0117 966 5202

An international organization of bereaved parents offering friendship and understanding to other bereaved parents. Local branches nationally.

Eclipse Bereavement Care

Eclipse House
2 School Road
Wharton
Winsford
Cheshire
01606 554 584

One-to-one counselling project for adults and teenagers.

Foundation for Study of Infant Death

35 Belgrave Square
London SW1 8QB
0171 235 1721

Helpline service available.

Jewish Bereavement Counselling Service

PO Box 6748
London N3 3BX
0181 349 0839

Counselling by trained volunteers. Telephone helpline.

Lesbian and Gay Bereavement Project

AIDS Education Unit
Vaughan M Williams Centre
Colindale Hospital
London NW9 5HG
0181 200 0511

Advice, support, and counselling for bereaved gay men, lesbians, and their families and friends. Education. Telephone helpline (evenings).

National Association of Bereavement Services

20 Norton Folgate
London E1 6DB
0171 247 1080
Admin/fax: 0171 247 0617

Provider of information, conferences and workshops. Membership and newsletter by subscription.

Nelson's Journey

01603 414104

A new charity, based on the Winston's Wish model, which aims to offer a county-wide service in Norfolk.

Northampton Children's Bereavement Project

c/o Social Work Dept
General Hospital
Cliftonville
Northampton NN1 5BD
01604 634700 ext. 5564 (Rosemary Weston)

Groupwork counselling with bereaved children, running in blocks through the year. Educational videos available for bereavement groups.

S.A.M.M.

Survivors after Murder and Manslaughter
128 Bowler Street
Kensington
Liverpool L6 6AD
0151 263 6767

Advice, support and information for families affected by murder/manslaughter.

SANDS – Stillbirth and Neonatal Death Society

28 Portland Place
London W1N 4DE
0171 436 5881

SHADO

120 Stonebridge Lane
Croxteth
Liverpool L14
0151 546 1141

Family support. Drugs advice. Advice, information and counselling for adults, young people and children.

St Christopher's Hospice

51–59 Lawrie Park Road
Sydenham SE26 6DZ
0181 778 9252

Includes a bookshop, with stock for adults and children.

Orchard Project

Orchard House
Fenwick Terrace
Jesmond
Newcastle NE2 2JQ
0191 281 5024

Barnardo's children's bereavement project.

Treetops – Corrymeela Community
   8 Upper Crescent
   Belfast BT7 1NT
   01232 325008
   Fax: 01232 315385
Support and information about bereavement service in Northern Ireland.

Wave and Loss
* Widows Against Violence Empower
* Loved Ones Say Stop
   523 Antrim Road
   Belfast BT15 3BS
   01232 779922
Groups to support victims of NI Troubles and violence.

Winston's Wish
   Palliative Care Team
   Gloucester Royal Hospital
   Great Western Road
   Gloucester GL1 3NN
   01452 528 555 ext. 4377
Grief support programme for adults and children: USA-style camps, after-school groups, individual work.

Useful Internet Web Sites

The Internet is increasingly being used for communicating information and for discussion groups. Its value is that local and national boundaries are so easily overcome, permitting easy access to professionals and academics worldwide. Even though many people will not have Internet access at home or in the workplace, it can still be worthwhile making a visit to a cybercafé. The following is a list of some of the web sites which were used in researching this book – the list is by no means exhaustive. As with any other form of publication, we are not suggesting that these sites should be read uncritically, but feel that the reader will find much of interest. Most sites have search facilities to search its contents, as well as links to related material on other sites.

Journals

Australasian Journal of Disaster and Trauma Studies
   http://www.massey.ac.nz/~trauma/

British Medical Journal
   http://www.bmj.com/index.html

Children's magazines – too many to list!
Try www.yahoo.co.uk and look under Magazines/Society and culture.

Health Service Journal
   http://www.hsj.macmillan.com
NHS health and management issues.

Bereavement and Disasters

Bereavement Services
   http://www.bereavement.net
Ontario, Canada.

Center for Loss
   http://www.centerforloss.com

Child Page
   http://hospicefoundation.org/childpg.htm
Collections of original writings on children and grief.

Depression Central
    http://www.psychom.net/depression.central.grief.html

Disasters: how to cope
    http://www.health.gov.au/nhmrc/publicat/pamphlet/mh7pam.htm
Australian government information leaflet.

The Disaster Center
    http://www.disastercenter.com/home2.htm
Includes links to disaster, trauma and relevant childhood information.

The Global Health Disaster Network
    http://ghd.uic.net/
Canadian and USA sites, include listings of disaster networks, news sources,
and list of worldwide journal editions which contain disaster information.

Grief, loss and recovery
    http://www.erichad.com/grief

Growthhouse
    http://www.growthhouse.org/famgrie1.htm
Chatroom, online bookstore, links to AIDS, terminal illness, hospices.

Hospice Net
    http://www.hospicenet.org/

London Bereavement Network
    http://www.bereavement.demon.co.uk
Includes links to bereavement services on the Internet.

Parenting advice on family traumas
    http://childparenting.tqn.com/msub5d.htm

Teenagers and bereavement
    http://dying.miningco.com/msub22.htm

General information

Barnardo's
    http://www.barnardos.org.uk
Children's charity.

Charities Aid Foundation (CAF) 'Charitynet'
    http://www.charitynet.org/
Latest information for UK charities – funding, research, and so on.

Centre for Europe's Children
    http://eurochild.gla.ac.uk/
Designed to influence policy-makers toward the UN Convention on the
Rights of the Child.

Children's Society
  http://www.the-childrens-society.org.uk
Children's charity.

EF Schumacher Society
  http://www.schumachersociety.org
Library and publications.

Mailbase discussion lists – for scholarly debate and exchange of information.
  http://www.mailbase.ac.uk/lists/death-soccon
  http://www.mailbase.ac.uk/lists/natural-hazards-disasters

(UK) National Council for Voluntary Organizations
  http://www.vois.org.uk/ncvo/

NCH Action For Children
  http://www.nchafc.org.uk
Children's charity.

NSPCC
  http://www.nspcc.org.uk
Children's charity.

UK Government Information Service – index
  http://www.open.gov.uk/index/orgindex.htm
Many useful links to government departments, local government, and non-governmental bodies.

Reading Lists for Children and Adults

Books for children
For under 5 years and 5–8 years

Johnson, J. (1982) *Where's Jess?* Omaha, Nebraska: Centering Corporation.

Nystram, C. (1981) *What Happens when we Die?* Moody Press.

Sims, A. (1986) *Am I Still a Sister?* New York: Big A.

Varley, S. (1985) *Badger's Parting Gifts.* Oxford: Lion Publishing.

Wilhelm, H. (1985) *I'll always Love You.* London: Hodder and Stoughton.

Williams, M. (1975) *The Velveteen Rabbit.* New York: Avon Books.

For 5–11 years

Althea (1982) *When Uncle Bob Died.* London: Dinosaur Publications..

Buscaglia, L. (1982) *Fall of Freddie the Leaf.* USA: Charles Slack.

Kubler-Ross, E. (1982) *Remember the Secret.* USA: Celestial Arts.

Nugee, R. (1971) *William is our Brother.* Mother's Union.

Stickney, D. (1982) *Waterbugs and Dragonflies.* London: Mowbray.

Viorst, J. (1971) *Tenth Good Thing about Barney.* New York: Athenaeum.

White, P. (1976) *What's Happened to Auntie Jean?* Scripture Union.

For 8–11 years

Mellonie and Ingpen (1983) *Lifetimes: A Beautiful Way to Explain Death to Children.* London: Bantam Books.

White, E.B. (1952) *Charlotte's Web.* London: Puffin.

For 8–15 years

Milne, K. (1977) *A Time to Die.* Hove, East Sussex: Wayland Publishers.

For 12–15 years

Ball, M. (1976) *Death.* Oxford: Oxford University Press.

Greene, C. (1976) *Beat the Turtle Drum.* New York: The Viking Press.

Krementz, J. (1981) *How it Feels when a Parent Dies.* New York: Alfred Knopf.

LaTour, K. (1972) *For Those who Live.* Omaha, Nebraska: Centering Corporation.

Levy, E.L. (1982) *Children are Not Paper Dolls.* USA: Mark Publications.

Little, J. (1980) *Mama's Going to Buy you a Mocking Bird.* London: Puffin.

Richter, E. (1986) *Losing Someone you Love.* New York: Putnam's.

Books about children's mourning

For parents and other adults

Jewett, C. (1982, 1984) *Helping Children to Cope with Separation and Loss.* Harvard: Harvard Universtity Press.

More suitable for professionals than parents.

Kirkwood, N. (1984) *A Child's Questions about Death.* Baptist Chaplaincy Care Service.

Kubler-Ross, E. (1983) *On Children and Death.* USA: Collier Books.

LaTour, K. (1972) *For Those who Live.* Omaha, Nebraska: Centering Corporation.

Torrie, A. (1978) *When Children Grieve.* Cruse.

Wynnejones, P. (1985) *Children, Death and Bereavement.* Scripture Union.

For parents and children

Althea, (1988) *When Uncle Bob Died.* London: Dinosaur Publications.

Branfield, J. (1981) *The Fox in Winter.* Oxford: Lions Publishing.

Bryant-Mole, K. (1992) *Death – What's Happening?* Hove, East Sussex: Wayland Publishers.

Buchanan Smith, D. (1987) *A Taste of Blackberries.* London: Puffin.

Capacchione, L. (1989) *The Creative Journal for Children.* Boston and Shaftesbury: Shambhala.

Couldrick, A. (1988) *Grief and Bereavement: Understanding Children.* Sobell Publications.

Couldrick, A. (1991) *When your Mum or Dad has Cancer.* Sobell Publications.

Heegaard, M. (1988) *Facilitator Guide for 'When Someone Very Special Dies…'* Woodland Press.

Hoy, L. (1983) *Your Friend Rebecca.* London: Bodley Head.

Krementz, J. (1991) *How it Feels when a Parent Dies.* London: Gollancz.

Little, J. (1980) *Mama's Going to Buy you a Mockingbird.* London: Puffin.

Paterson, K. (1980) *Bridge to Terabithia.* London: Puffin.

Shawe, M. (ed) (1992) *Enduring, Sharing, Loving. For all those Affected by the Death of a Child.* Darton: Longman and Todd.

St Christopher's Hospice (S.W. dept) (1989) *Someone special has died.*

Sims, A. (1986) *Am I Still a Sister?* New York: Big A.

Stickney, D. (1984) *Waterbugs and Dragonflies.* London: Mowbray.

Varley, S. (1985) *Badger's Parting Gifts.* London: Picture Lions.

Wilkinson, T. (1991) *The Death of a Child: A Book for Families.* London: Julie MacRae Books.

Bibliography

Books

Acheson, Sir Donald (1998) *Independent Inquiry into Inequalities in Health*. London: HMSO.
A summary of social policy, social and economic inequality and health inequality, following from the Black Report and *The Health Divide*.

Altschul, S. (1988) *Childhood Bereavement and its Aftermath*. Madison Connecticut: International University Press.

Ayalon, O. (1988) *Rescue! Community Oriented Preventative Education for Coping with Stress*. Haifa, Israel: Nord Publications (also 1992: Ellicot City: Chevron Publications).

Bandura, A. (1986) *Social Foundation of Thought and Action*. Englewood Cliffs, New Jersey: Prentice Hall.

Barnard, P. and Kane, M. (1995) 'Voices from the crowd – stories from the Hillsborough Football Stadium Disaster'. In S. Smith and M. Pennells (eds) *Interventions with Bereaved Children*. London: Jessica Kingsley.

Bee, H. (1992) *The Developing Child, 6th Edition*. London: Harper and Row.
Includes reference to young children's 'magical thinking', for example that they 'caused' a death.

Black, D. and Young, B. (1995) 'Bereaved children: risk and preventative intervention'. In B. Raphael and G. Burrows (eds) *Handbook of Studies on Preventive Psychiatry*. Amsterdam: Elsevier.

Black, Sir Douglas (1980) *Inequalities in Health* ('The Black Report'). London: HMSO.

Brown, G.W. and Harris, T. (1978) *Social Origins of Depression*. London: Tavistock.
Includes finding that children under the age of 11 who lose their mother are more at risk.

Douglas, T. (1991) *A Handbook of Common Groupwork Problems*. London: Routledge.

Dwivedi, K.N. (1994) *Group Work with Children and Adolescents: A Handbook*. London: Jessica Kingsley.
Includes a description of children's age-related stages of understanding/ conceptualizing death.

Dyregrov, A. (1991) *Grief in Children: A Handbook for Adults*. London: Jessica Kingsley.
Includes a description of children's age-related stages of understanding/ conceptualizing death. Hiding facts can cause anxieties and fantasies to develop.

Field, M. and Lohr, K. (1992) *Guidelines for Clinical Practice. From Development to Use.* Washington: National Academic Press.
Promotion of empirical, evidence-based practice.

Friedson, E. (1970) *Profession of Medicine: A Study of the Sociology of Applied Knowledge.* New York: Dodd, Mead and Company.
A study of the interaction, and conflict and negotiation, between medical professionals and patients.

Garmezy, N. (1985) 'Stress resilient children: The search for protective factors'. In J. Stevenson (ed) *Recent Research in Developmental Psychopathogy.* Oxford: Pergamon Press.

Grollman, E. (1991) *Talking About Death: Dialogue Between a Parent and Child, 3rd Edition.* Boston MA: Beacon.
The Western world's romantic idealization of childhood has led to particular problems, including inability to talk with children about death and suffering, therefore, they are kept away from facts by adults who wish to protect them. 'Traumatic experiences belong to both adulthood and childhood.'

Grotberg, E. (1995) *A Guide to Promoting Resilience in Children.* The Hague: Bernard van Leer Foundation, Netherlands.

Heidegger, M. (1927) *Being and Time.* Translated by John MacQuarrie and Oswald Robinson (1962). Oxford: Basil Blackwell.

Hendriks, J.H. (1993) *When Father Kills Mother: Guiding Children Through Trauma and Grief.* London: Routledge in association with the Royal College of Psychiatrists.

Hodgkinson, P.E. and Stewart, M. (1991) *Coping with a Catastrophe – a Handbook of Disaster Management.* London: Routledge.

Johnson, K. (1989) *Trauma in the Lives of Children.* Basingstoke: Macmillan.

Judd, D. (1989) *Give Sorrow Words.* London: Free Association Books.

Katon, W. and Kleinman, A. (1981) 'Doctor–patient negotiation and other social science strategies in patient care'. In L. Eisberg and A. Kleinman (eds) *The Relevance of Social Science to Medicine.* Dordrecht: Reidel.

Knight, B. (1993) *Voluntary Action.* London: HMSO.
An HMSO/CENTRIS research project into the nature of voluntary activity in the 1990s, the philosophies of voluntary organizations (philanthropic and self-help), and the social, economic and political issues confronting them.

Van der Kolk, B.A. (undated) *Psychological Trauma.* Washington DC: American Psychiatric Press Inc.

Kotler, P. and Roberto, E. (1989) *Social Marketing. Strategies for Changing Public Behaviour.* New York: Free Press.

Kubler-Ross, E. (1969) *On Death and Dying.* London: Routledge.

Lothian Community Relations Council (1978) *Religions and Cultures: A Guide to Patients' Beliefs and Customs for Health Service Staff.* Edinburgh: Lothian Community Relations Council.

Lowe, R. (1993) *The Welfare State in Britain Since 1945.* London: Macmillan.

A social history of the British welfare state, covering health, education, and the statutory and voluntary social services.

Maines, B. and Robinson, G. (1988) *B/G Steem – A Self Esteem Scale*. Bristol: Lame Duck Publications.

McKnight, J.L. (1984) *John Deere and The Bereavement Counselor*. Great Barrington, MA (USA): EF Schumacher Foundation.
Presented by John L. McKnight (Center for Urban Affairs and Policy Research, Northwestern University, Evanston, Illinois) at 4th Annual EF Schumacher Lectures, Foote School, New Haven. October 1984. Copies are available from the EF Schumacher Society, 140 Jug End Road, Great Barrington, MA 01230, USA, for US $5.50 inc. p+p.

Mullins, L.J. (1993 Third Edition) *Management and Organizational Behaviour Third Edition*. London: Pitman.
A textbook of management and organization theory and practice.

Newburn, T. (1993) *Disaster and After – Social Work in the Aftermath of Disaster*. London: Jessica Kingsley.

Osterweis, F.M. (1984) *Bereavement: Reactions, Consequences, and Care*. Washington, DC: National Academy Press.

Papadato, D. and Papadato, C. (eds) (1991) *Children and Death*. New York: Hemisphere.
Includes a description of children's age-related stages of understanding/ conceptualizing death.

Perkin, H. (1989) *The Rise of Professional Society: England since 1880*. London: Routledge.
A popular and landmark work of social history, which examines the emergence and triumph of professionalism during the twentieth century.

Pervin, L. (1970) *Personality*. New York: John Wiley and Sons.

Peterson, J. and Files, L. (1989) 'The marriage of art therapy and psychodrama'. In Wadeson, H. Durkin, J. and Perach, D. (eds) *Advances in Art Therapy*. New York: John Wiley and Sons.

Rao Punnkollu, N. (1990) *Recent Advances in Crisis Intervention*. Huddersfield: International Institute of Crisis Intervention and Community Psychiatry Publications.

Raphael, B. (1986) *When Disaster Strikes*. London: Hutchinson.

Rogers, E. (1983) *Diffusion of Innovations*. New York: Free Press.
Social interaction and changes in human behaviour; the role of significant people.

Rushton, L. *Death Customs*. Hove: Wayland, 1992. (the Understanding Religions Series).

Shears, J. (1995) 'Managing a tragedy in a secondary school'. In S. Smith and M. Pennells (eds) *Interventions with Bereaved Children*. London: Jessica Kingsley Publishers.

Smith, S. and Pennells, M. (1994) *The Forgotten Mourners: Guidelines for Working with Bereaved Children.* London: Jessica Kingsley Publishers.

Smith, S. and Pennells, M. (eds) (1995) *Interventions with Bereaved Children.* London: Jessica Kingsley Publishers.
Includes contributions from Peta Hemmings (communication through play), Pennells and Smith, Stokes and Crossley (Winston's Wish), John Shears (incident at Steeley Street School), use of drama, art, group work, one-to-one work. Foreword by William Yule.

Steiner, G. (1978) *Heidegger.* London: Fontana Modern Masters.
An appraisal of Martin Heidegger's philosophy and influence.

Steinhardt, L. (1989) 'Six starting points in art therapy with children'. In Wadeson, H. Durkin, J. and Perach, D. (eds) *Advances in Art Therapy.* New York: John Wiley and Sons.

Stock Whitaker, D. and Archer, J.L. (1989) *Research by Social Workers: Capitalizing on Experience.* Study Guide no.9. London: CCETSW.

Stokes, J. and Crossley, D. (1996) *Winston's Wish – A Grief Support Programme for Children, Progress Report 1993–95.* Gloucester: Winston's Wish.

Stokes, J., Wyer, S. and Crossley, D. (1996) *The Challenge of Evaluating a Child Bereavement Programme.* Gloucester: Winston's Wish.

Tizard, B. and Varma, V. (eds) (1992) *Vulnerability and Resilience in Human Development.* London: Jessica Kingsley Publishers.
Vulnerability and resilience are explored in a wide range of situations.

Townsend, P. and Davidson, N. (1992) 'The Black Report'. In P. Townsend, N. Davidson and M. Whitehead (eds) *Inequalities in Health.* London: Penguin Books.

Townsend, P., Davidson, N. and Whitehead, M. (eds) (1992) *Inequalities in Health.* London: Penguin Books.
Update on the original findings of the Black Report of 1980, drawing together links of poverty and material deprivation with ill-health and mortality.

Wadsworth, Y. (1991) *Everyday Evaluation on the Run.* Melbourne, Australia: Action Research Issues Association Inc.

Whitehead, M. (1987) 'The Health Divide'. In P. Townsend, N. Davidson and M. Whitehead (eds) (1992) *Inequalities in Health.* London: Penguin Books.

Worden, W. (1991) *Grief Counselling and Grief Therapy.* London: Tavistock/Routledge.

Yule, W. and Gold, A. (1993) *Coping with Crises in Schools – Wise Before the Event.* Calouste Gulbenkian Foundation, London.

Zambelli, G.C., Johns Clark, E. and Heegaard, M. (1989) 'Art therapy for bereaved children'. In Wadeson, H. Durkin, J. and Perach, D. (eds) *Advances in Art Therapy.* New York: John Wiley and Sons.
Experiencing a significant loss at an early stage creates intense confusion and pain; intervention is required to prevent long-term psychological problems.

Art therapy is an effective means of identifying misconceptions and issues of conflict, thereby promoting fuller expression for feelings of grief. Art therapy is therefore emerging as a viable new intervention for working with bereaved children.

Articles in journals and periodicals

All publications are United Kingdom unless otherwise stated.

Abrams, R. (1993) 'Parental bereavement: its effect on young people'. *Childright 101*, 15–17.

Alexander, D.A. and Wells, W. (1991) 'Reactions of police officers to body-handling after a major disaster: a before and after comparison'. *British Journal of Psychiatry 159*, 547–555.

Baines, S. (1994) 'Life after death'. *Care Weekly*, 3 June, 13.
Report on Liverpool Children's Project and its group work with children.

Bennett, G. and Roud, S. (1997) 'Death customs'. In *Mortality 2, 3*, 221–238.
The changing face of folklore and death customs.

Beswick, G. and Bean, D. (1996) 'Group work for bereaved children: a team approach'. *Nursing Standard 10*, 41, 3 July, 35–37.

Bhaduri, R. (1991) 'A sense of karma'. *Social Work Today*, 2 May.
Assessing the usefulness of the *Bhagavad Gita* to grief counselling … spiritual approach to life and death.

Bisson, J.I. and Cullum, M. (1994) 'Group therapy for bereaved children'. *ACCP Review and Newsletter 16*, 3, 130–138.
Link between 'disturbance' in the parents and in the children after a trauma.

Black, D. (1996) 'Childhood bereavement'. *British Medical Journal 312*, 15 June, 1496.
Consultant child and adolescent psychiatrist, Traumatic Stress Clinic, London W1P 1LB.

Breier, A., Kelsoe, J.R., Kirwin, P.D., Beller, S.A., Wolkowitz, O.M. and Pickard, D. (1988) 'Early parental loss and development of adult psychopathology'. *Archives of General Psychiatry 45*, 11, 982–993.

Brogan, C., Pickard, D., Gray, A., Fairman, S. and Hill, A. (1998) 'The use of out of hours health services: a cross sectional survey'. *British Medical Journal 316*, 14 February, 524–527.

Burman, S. and Allen-Meares, P. (1994) 'Neglected victims of murder: children's witness to parental homicide'. *Social Work 39*, 1, 28–34.

Capewell, E. (1992) 'Disaster – how can schools respond?' *National Council of Parent–Teacher Associations*, March 1992, 37–41.

Clegg, F. (1988) 'Disasters: can psychologists help the survivors?' *The Psychologist*, April 1988.

Day, P. (1991) 'Letting go'. *Social Work Today*, 2 May.

Dobson, R. (1995) 'Single minded: counselling anyone with a life threatening cancer is never easy, but single parents pose particular problems'. *Community Care*, 20 April, 21.

Dominica, F. (1987) 'Reflections on death in childhood: personal paper'. *British Medical Journal 294*, 10 January, 108–110.

Van Eerdewegh, M.M., Clayton, P.J. and van Eerdewegh, P. (1985) 'The bereaved child: variables influencing early psychopathology'. *British Journal of Psychiatry 147*.
Very much a statistical medical-model approach. Notes that children's school performance can deteriorate after a bereavement.

Francis, J. (1993) 'Overcoming the taboo'. *Community Care*, 27 May, 23.
Article on Liverpool Children's Project, children and bereavement.

Froggatt, K. (1997) 'Rites of passage and the hospice culture'. In *Mortality 2*, 2 July, 123–136.
Argues that the hospice culture is informed by a rites-of-passage model from social anthropology.

Green, J. (1989) 'Death with dignity'. *Nursing Times 85*, 5–9.
Series of articles describing different cultures' approaches to death and dying – Islam, Hinduism, Sikhism, Judaism, Buddhism.

Green, J. and Britten, N. (1998) 'Education and debate: qualitative research and evidence based medicine'. *British Medical Journal 316*, 1230–1232.
Commentary on the problems of qualitative and quantitative evidence for effectiveness of clinical interventions, re the debate on evidence-based medicine.

Grimshaw, J., Freemantle, N., Wallace, S., Russel, I., Hurwitz, B., Watt, I., Long, A. and Sheldon, T. (1995) 'Developing and implementing practice guidelines'. In *Quality in Health Care 4*, 55–64.

Grist, R. and Woodall, S. Joseph (1998) 'Social science versus social movements: the origins and natural history of debriefing'. *The Australasian Journal of Disaster and Trauma Studies*. Vol: 1998–1.

Haines, A. and Jones, R. (1994) 'Implementing findings of research'. *British Medical Journal 308*, 1488–1492.

Hardwick, C. (1988) 'The last taboo'. *Community Care*, 8 September, 24.
Do dying children get a raw deal from social workers?

Hemmings, P. (1990) 'Dealing with death'. *Community Care*, 12 April, 16–17.
Bereavement practitioner, creator of the 'All About Me' board game.

Jeffrey, P. and Lansdown, R. (1993) 'The role of the special school in the care of the dying child'. *Bereavement Care 12*, 2. (Reprinted from *Developmental Medicine and Child Neurology* 1982, 24, 693–696).

Kitchener, S. and Pennells, M. (1990) 'A bereavement group for children'. *Bereavement Care 9*, 3, 30–31.

Kranzler, E.M., Shaffer, D., Wasserman, G. and Davies, M. (1990) 'Early childhood bereavement'. *Journal of the American Academy of Child and Adolescent Psychiatry 29*, 4, July (USA).
From the Department of Psychiatry, Columbia University College of Physicians and Surgeons, New York State Psychiatric Institute. Reprint requests to Dr Kranzler, Division of Child Psychiatry, Columbia University, New York State Psychiatric Institute, 722 W 168 St, NY 10032.

Lindemann, E. (1944) 'Symptomatology and management of acute grief'. *American Journal of Psychiatry 151*, 6, 155 (USA).
Some interesting comments about grief and loss during World War II.

Martin, A. (1992) 'Death and dolphins'. *Young People Now*, May, 18–19.
The Hillsborough Project and Freddie the dolphin; the methodology of using group work to introduce children to new experiences to rebuild their confidence and self-esteem.

McFarlane, A.C. (1989) 'The treatment of post-traumatic stress disorder'. *British Journal of Medical Psychiatry 62*, 81–90.

McNamara, B. (1997) 'The stereotypical fallacy: a comparison of Anglo and Chinese Australians' thoughts about facing death'. In *Mortality 2*, 2, 149–161.
Examines the cultural differences between these two groups, and the implications for practitioners working with patients/clients.

Moran, C. and Massam, M. (1997) 'An evaluation of humour in emergency work'. *The Australasian Journal of Disaster and Trauma Studies*. Vol:1997–3.

Olowu, A.A. (1990) 'Helping children cope with death'. *Early Child Development and Care 61*, 119–123.

Pearson, R.E. (1983) 'Support groups: a conceptualization'. *The Personnel and Guidance Journal*, February (USA), 361–364.

Pithers, D. (1990) 'Acting fair'. *Nursing Times 90*, 8, 32.
Comments that the power of adults and parents is often assumed to be used for the best, but it may not be so – need to ask 'in whose interests' a decision is being made.

Redding, D. (1990) 'The Bridge Builder'. *Community Care*, 18 January, 18–19.

Rutter, M. (1981) 'Stress, coping and development, some issues and some questions'. *Journal of Child Psychology and Psychiatry 22*, 323–356.

Rutter, M. (1987) 'Psychosocial resilience and protective mechanisms'. *American Journal of Orthopsychiatry 57*, 3, 316–331 (USA).
The concept of mechanisms that protect people against the psychological risks associated with adversity is discussed in relation to four main processes: (1) Reduction of risk impact; (2) reduction of negative chain reactions; (3) establishment and maintenance of self-esteem and self-efficacy; (4) opening up of opportunities.

Rutter, M. (1999) 'Resilience concepts and findings: Implications for family therapy.' *Journal of Family Therapy 21*, 2, 119–144.

Schilling, R.F., Koh, N., Abramovitz, R. and Gilbert, L. (1992) 'Bereavement groups for inner city children'. *Research on Social Work Practice 2*, 3, 405–419 (USA).

Small, E. (1992) 'Good grief'. *Social Work Today*, 19 March, 18–19.
Northampton Children's Bereavement Project (Sue Smith and Margaret Pennells).

Smith, J. (1991) 'The Hillsborough Disaster: the personal account of a post-disaster worker'. *CPNJ*, April.

Stallard, P. and Law, F. (1994) 'The psychological effects of traumas on children'. *Children and Society 8*, 2, 89–97.
There is growing evidence to demonstrate that children involved in traumatic events suffer prolonged and significant psychological distress although adults have been found to consistently deny, underrate or fail to recognize their severity.

Therapy Weekly (1991) 'Do not blame the victims of disaster, therapists told'. *Therapy Weekly 17*, 42, May 9.

Walter, T. (1996a) 'New model of grief'. *Mortality 1*, 1, 7–25.
A hypothesis that grief and talking about the deceased helps to re-integrate or rehabilitate the dead person into survivors' ongoing lives.

Walter, T. (1996b) 'Ritualizing death in a consumer society'. *RSA Journal 144*, 32–40.

Wayne, P. (1998) 'Very bad boys'. *Prospect 26*, 72–73.
Written by a man serving 13 years for armed robbery: a commentary on the Jamie Bulger case, television, violence and mercy.

Wraith, R. (1987) 'Children and families in disaster'. Paper presented to Inaugural State Conference of the Australian Early Childhood Association Victorian Branch, 12 September 1987. Dept of Child and Family Psychiatry, Royal Children's Hospital, Melbourne, Australia.

Young, W. (1994) 'Contributions on childhood grief and bereavement'. *Bereavement Care Journal 13*, 3, 33–34.
Older girls who lose their mother may be a particularly vulnerable group.

Yule, W. (1989) 'The effects of disasters on children'. *Association of Child Psychology and Psychiatry Newsletter 11*, 6, 3–6.

Zambelli, G.C. and DeRosa, A.P. (1992) 'Bereavement support groups for school-age children: theory, intervention and case example'. *American Journal of Orthopsychiatry 62*, 4, 484–493 (USA).
Children's bereavement support groups can provide useful surrogate support for families when a parent dies, and may contribute new social meaning for this traumatic event.

Zambelli, G.C., Johns Clark, E.B.L. and de Jong, A.F. (1988) 'An interdisciplinary approach to clinical intervention for childhood bereavement'. *Death Studies 12*, 1, 41–50 (USA).

Newspaper articles

AIDS

Ballantyne, A. 'Learning to let mother go'. *The Sunday Times*, 22.2.98.
An 8-year-old girl who knows her mother may die of AIDS.

Thomas, D. 'The dark side of innocence'. *Guardian*, 26.11.97.
Children and young people. AIDS in Wales.

Beliefs

Erriker, C. 'What children believe before we tell them what to believe.' *Church Times Education*, 11.10.96.

Children / death in the family

Artley, A. 'I wish mum was still here'. *Sunday Telegraph*, 13.3.94.

Lacey, H. 'The loss adjusters'. *Independent on Sunday (Review)*, 22.6.97.
Winston's Wish Bereavement Project.

Mihill, C. 'Children hide long-term stress to avoid upsetting adults'. *Guardian*, 5.4.93.

Yule, W. 'Death of a sibling.' *Primary Forum*, 8.5.92.

Child care

Haselden, R. 'Lost children'. *Guardian*, 8.6.91, 15.7.91.
Child care consequences for children. Care in children's homes; children in care; homelessness.

Disasters

Ferguson, E. 'Once more with feeling'. *Observer*, 30.8.98; reply in 'Letters' 6.10.98.

Fox, M. 'Fountain fire – psychological effects ...' *Intermountain News* (California) 8.91.

Hillsborough

Arnott, H. 'Justice: Hillsborough's last victim?' *Legal Act*, 4.92.

Tansley, J. 'Tragedy families fight for justice'. *Liverpool Echo*, 2.8.89.

'Laying the ghosts to rest'. *Daily Post*, 13.4.94.

'Families demand inquest reopening'. *Guardian*, 15.4.92.

Northern Ireland

Breen, S. '"Daddy don't die" – killings in Northern Ireland.' *Childright 103*, 1/2.94.

Holland, M. 'The secrets of troubled minds'. *Observer*, 19.1.97.

Sharrock, D. 'The confusing anger of peace'. *Guardian*, 29.10.94.

Murder

Messud, C. 'Children who have seen too much'. *Guardian*, 15.4.92.
Murder in the family.

Persuad, R. 'Murderers in the family'. *Guardian*, 22.5.92.

Refugees

'Plea for easier passage for refugee children'. *Guardian,* undated (letter).

Beckett, F. 'Horror in the school bag'. *Guardian,* 5.5.92.
   Refugee children's memories.

Coward, R. 'A stolen childhood'. *Guardian,* 13.11.96.

Williams, T. 'Their lives in her hands'. *Guardian,* undated.
   Child war refugees.

Schools / education and bereavement

Beardmore, S. 'School exclusion – a reflection of failure?' *Childright,* 11.93.

MacKenzie, J. 'Life, death and meeting the parents'. *The Times Educational Supplement,* 8.5.92.

Marland, M. 'How to deal with death'. *Guardian,* 4.6.91.

Hugill, B. 'Teachers taught hard lesson in tragedy'. *Observer,* 3.4.94.
   Murder in school.

Suicide

'Suicide among young people'. *Liverpool Echo,* 21.5.92.
   Report, interview with Samaritans, pointers to suicide.

Neustatter, A. 'A death in the family'. *Guardian,* 29.3.94.

Survivors

Cooper, C. 'Fame from misfortune'. *The Times Higher Educational Supplement,* 14.97.
   Exploring the links between early loss and adult success – for example, Jeffrey Archer, Arthur Scargill.

Levy, A. 'Witness to cruelty'. *Guardian,* 26.4.94.
   Why are children subjected to trauma of giving evidence in court?

Mihill, C. 'Lost innocence of young survivors'. *Guardian,* 13.4.96.

Unpublished materials

Barnard, P. (1992) 'Presentation of LCP at Church House (Liverpool Diocese BSR)' 23.6.92. Manuscript, The Children's Society archive.
   Question and answer discussion of LCP's role and strategy, with Paul Barnard (LCP) and Steven Martin (Board of Social Responsibility).

Bone, A. (1990) 'Disaster team work: The Piper Alpha Outreach team'. Grampian Regional Council Social Work Department, 25 January 1990.

Craig, B. (ed) (1989) 'Disaster and opportunity'. Sheffield Area Bereavement Forum.
   Report of a day conference on the Hillsborough disaster and counselling services, 31.10.89.

Craig, B. (ed) (1990) 'Children and loss'. Sheffield Area Bereavement Forum.
   Report on Study Day on experience and needs of children facing loss, 5.6.90.

Grey, J. and Ellwand, D. (eds) (undated) 'Disasters'. Guidebook produced on behalf of the steering group of voluntary and statutory components of Liverpool Youth Services. Liverpool Youth Service.

Littlewood, L.J. (1990) 'Understanding parental grief'. Paper presented to Conference 'Children and Death', The Bereavement Trust, Stanford Hall, Loughborough, March 1990.

Ludford (undated) 'Loss of a parent'. Loughborough: The Bereavement Trust.

MacLeod, D. and Crate, R. (1990) 'Making sense out of chaos – the social work role in disaster: an introduction.' The Children's Society archive.
Printed materials from five-day residential training event, Burton Manor, Merseyside, 12–16 March 1990; includes 'Summary of Salient Points About Children's Coping'.

Martin, A. and Kane, M. (1993) 'Beginnings.' Manuscript, The Children's Society archive.
Information on Liverpool Children's Project early years.

Osborn, F. (1993) 'What is the value of the concept of resilience for policy and intervention?' Paper for the conference of the International Catholic Child Bureau's International Institute, New York, 31 October – 3 November 1993.

Smithson, J. (1989) 'Lockerbie' (unnamed paper dated 6.12.89). Manuscript, the Children's Society archive.

Wagner, P. (1990) 'Bereavement and loss – what can the teacher do when a death occurs?' From Children and Bereavement Course. The Children's Society archive.

'Respecting people's faiths and beliefs about birth and death.' Leeds Health For All (Leeds Joint Consultative Committee) December 1996. The Children's Society archive.

'Winston's Wish – a grief support programme for children. Progress Report 1993–95.' Gloucestershire: Winston's Wish 1996.

'Coping with children's reactions to earthquakes and other disasters' (1973) San Fernando Valley Child Guidance Clinic (USA).

'The Hillsborough project, team discussion' (undated). Manuscript, The Children's Society archive.

'Enniskillen Remembrance Day bombing 8.11.87.' Manuscript, The Children's Society archive.

Subject Index

Author Index